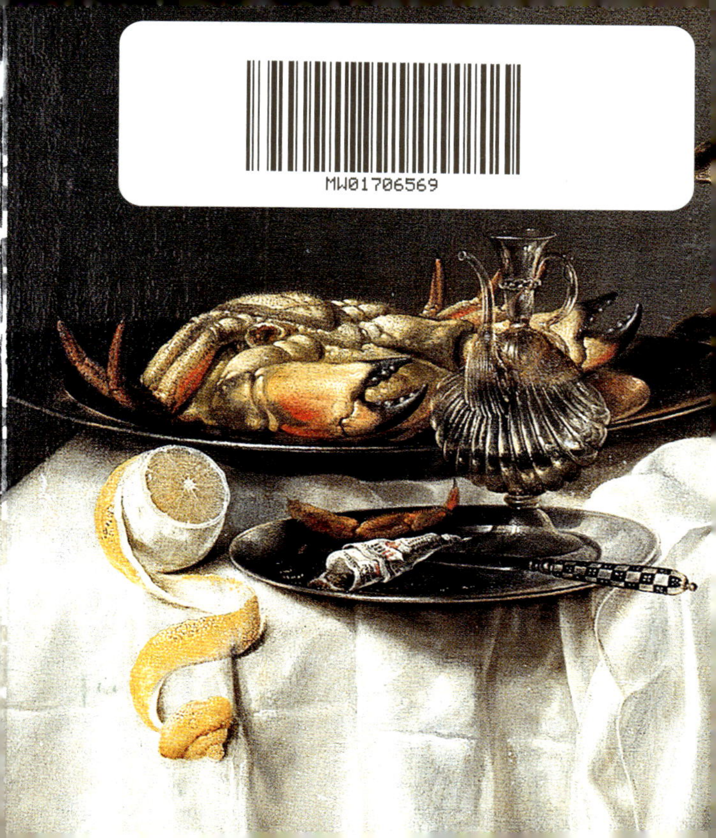

Editorial coordination of the series: Polina Yermakova

Editors: Elena Krutova, Anna Butyakova, Nina Zhutovsky

Designed by: Vladimir Yakovlev

Photography: Leonard Heifetz, Yuri Molodkovets, Vladimir Terebenin, Valery Zubarov

ISBN: 978-5-91208-332-7

THE HERMITAGE

Netherlandish
Flemish and
Dutch Painting

arca publishers

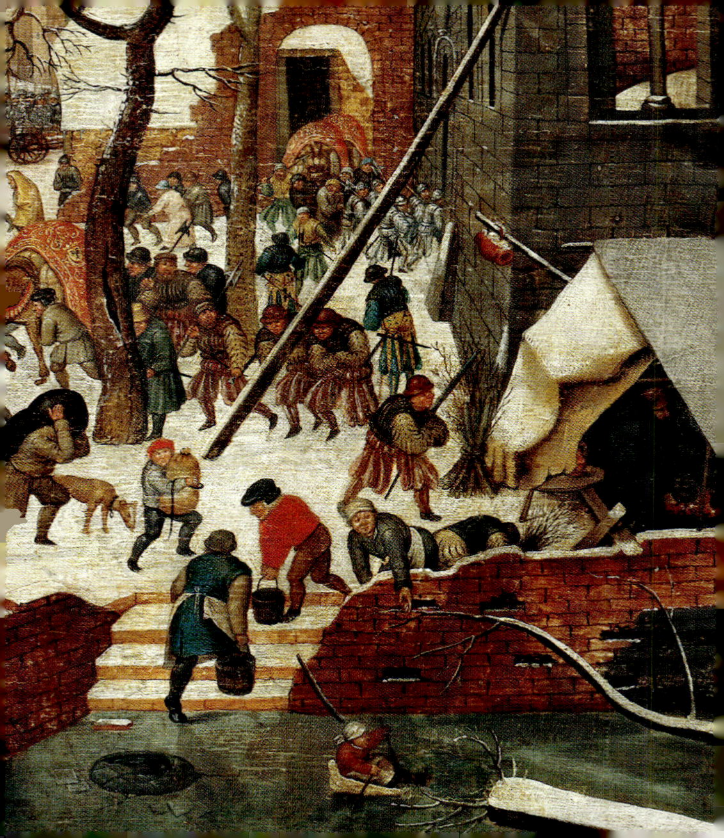

netherlands

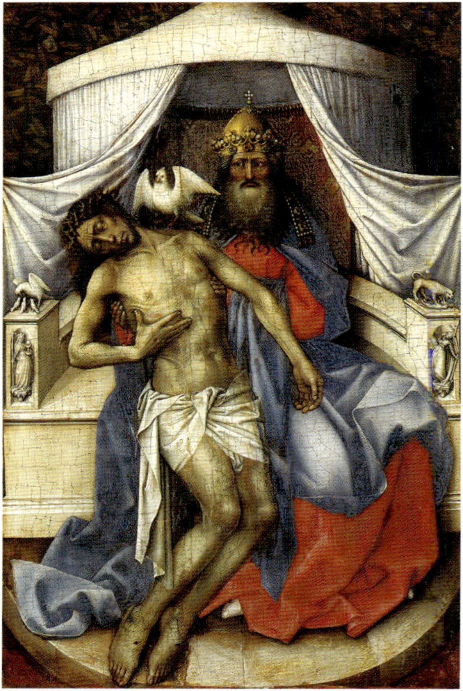

Robert Campin
(Master of Flemalle)
The Trinity. Diptych
Circa 1433–35
Netherlands

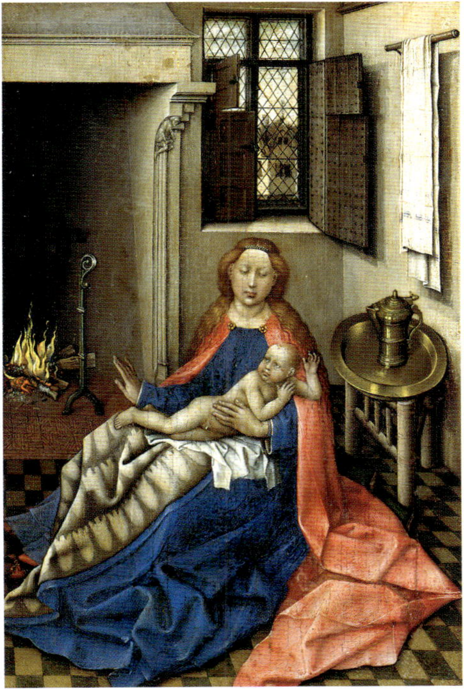

Robert Campin
(Master of Flemalle)
The Virgin and Child by a Fireplace. Diptych
Circa 1433–35
Netherlands

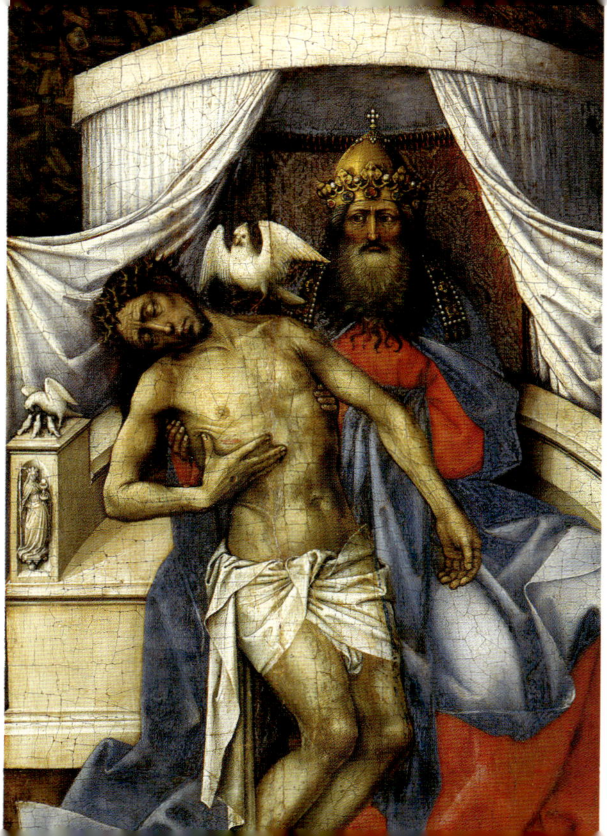

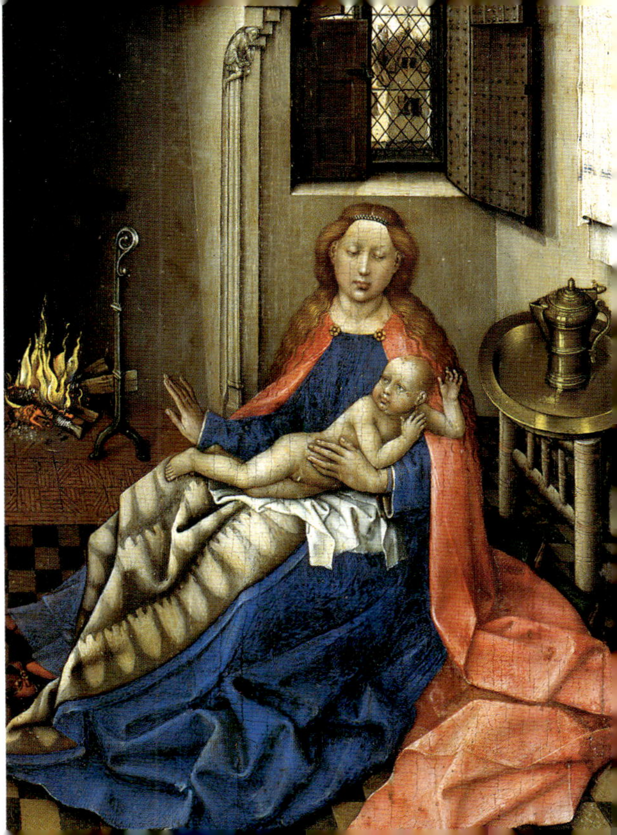

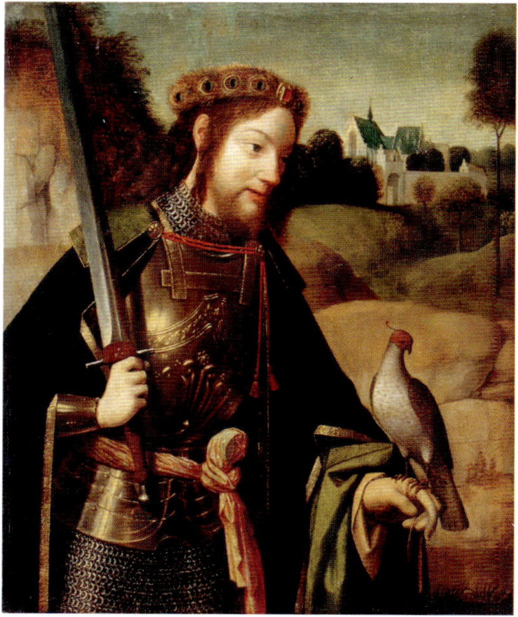

Geertgen Tot Sint Jans, Gerard (?)
St Bavo
Second half of the 15th century (?) Netherlands

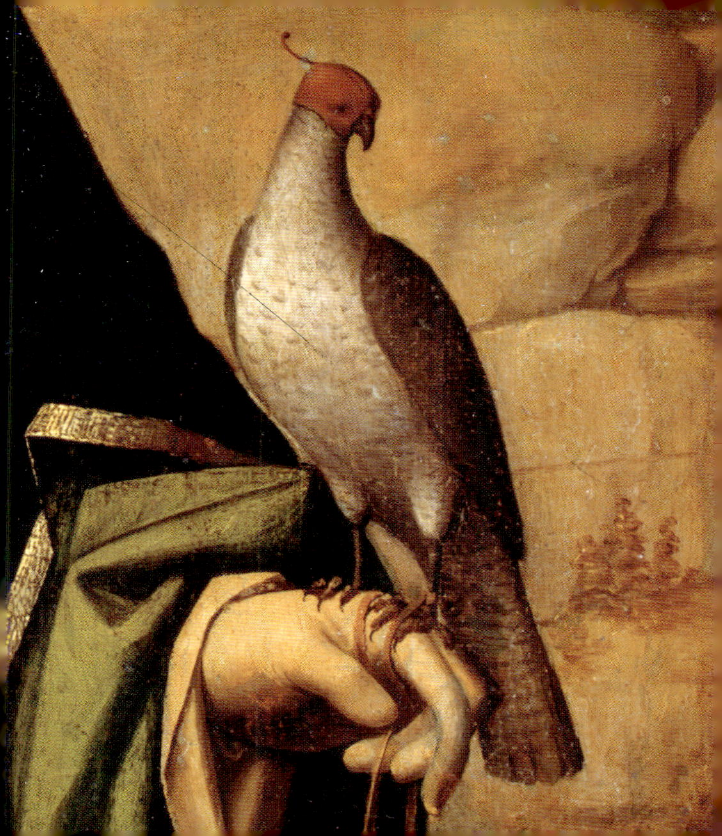

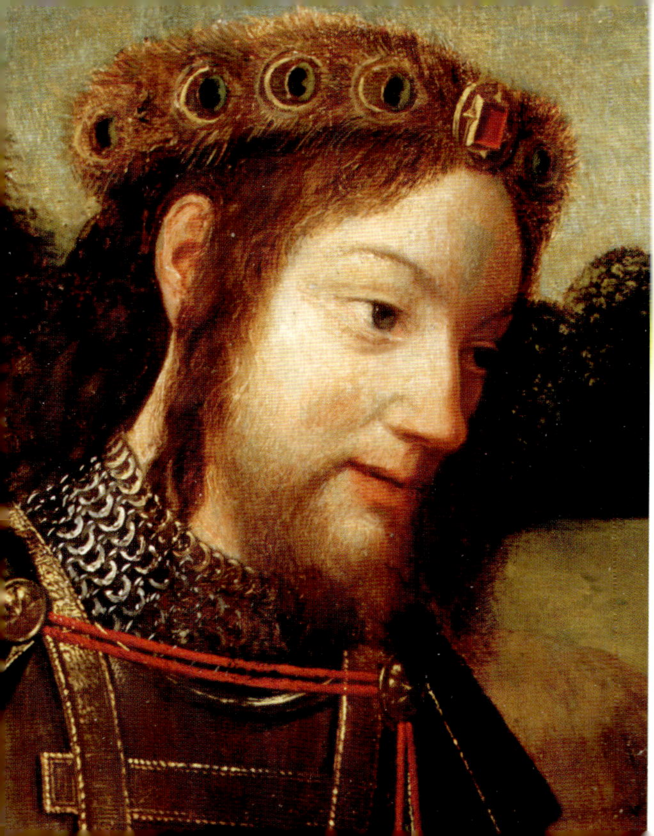

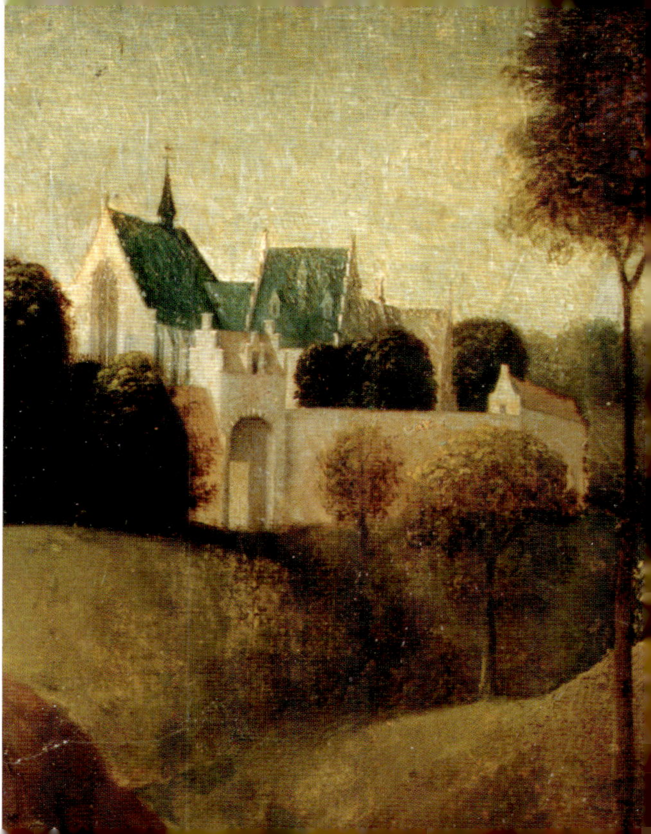

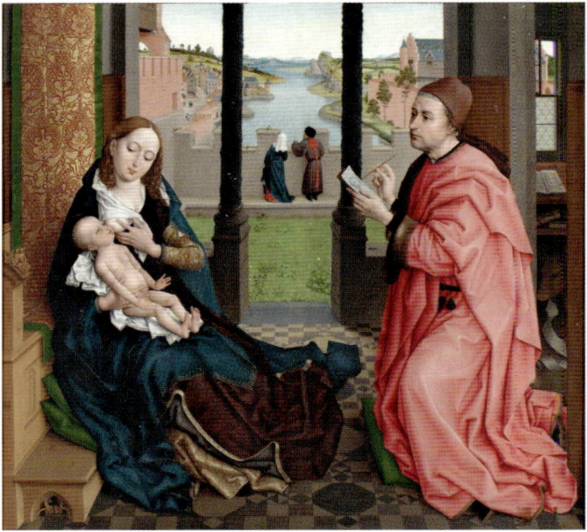

Rogier van der Weyden
St Luke Drawing the Virgin
15th century. Netherlands

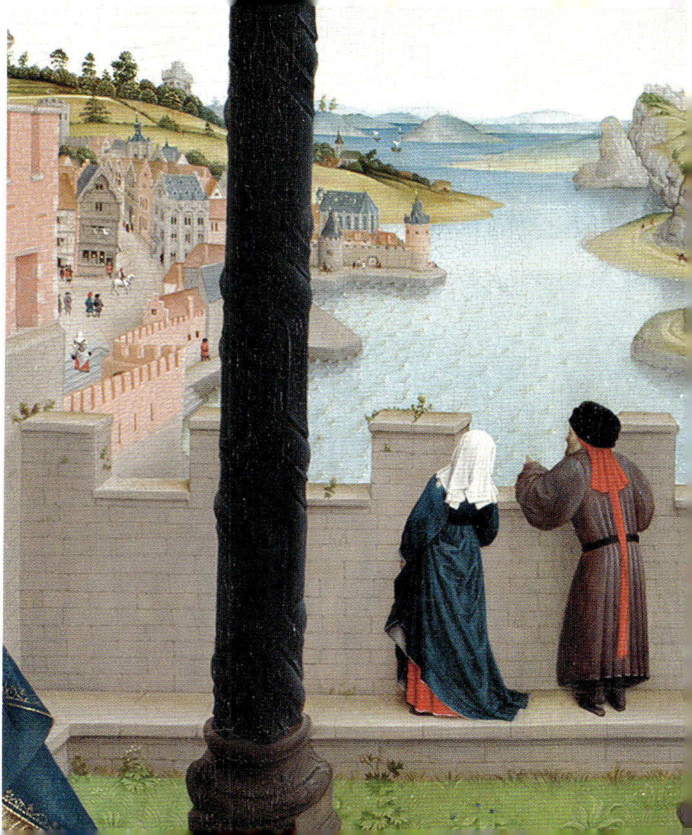

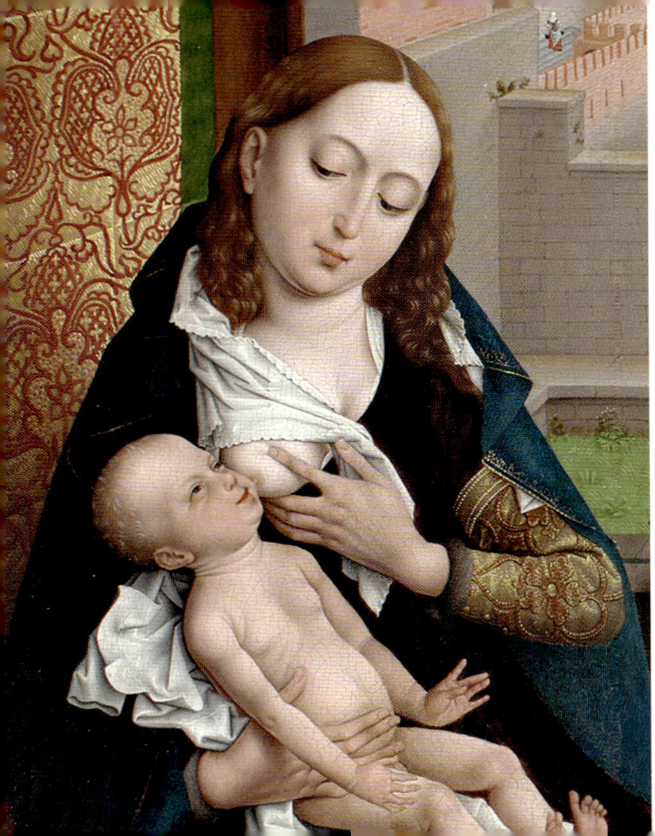

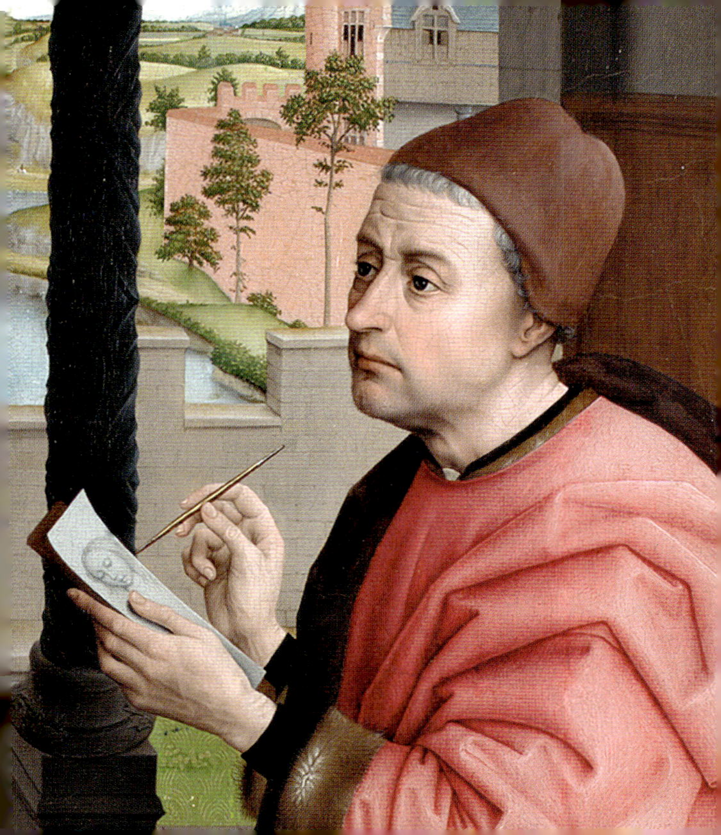

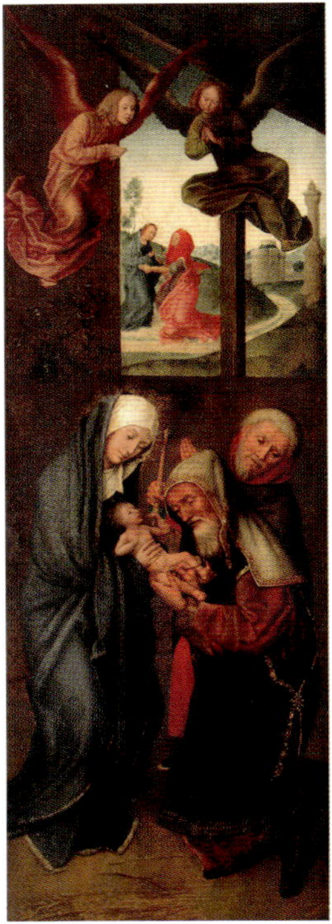

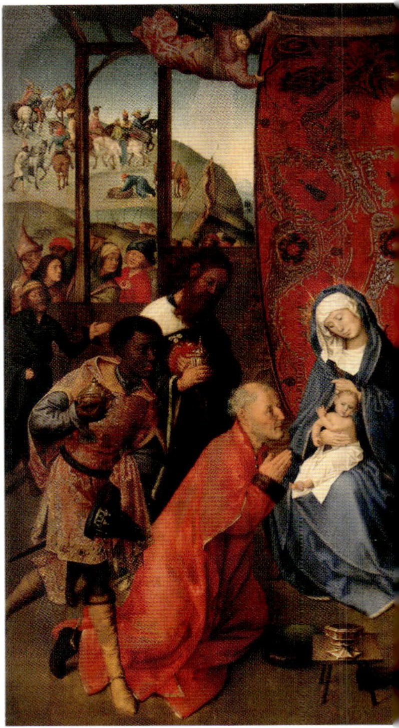

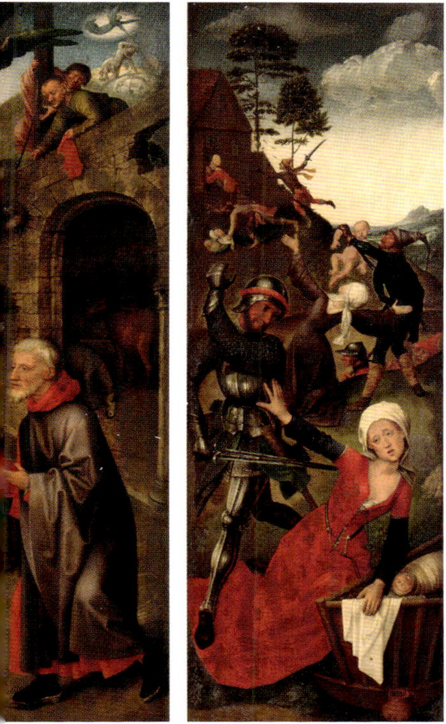

Hugo van der Goes
The Adoration of the Magi. Triptych
Second half of the 15th century. Netherlands

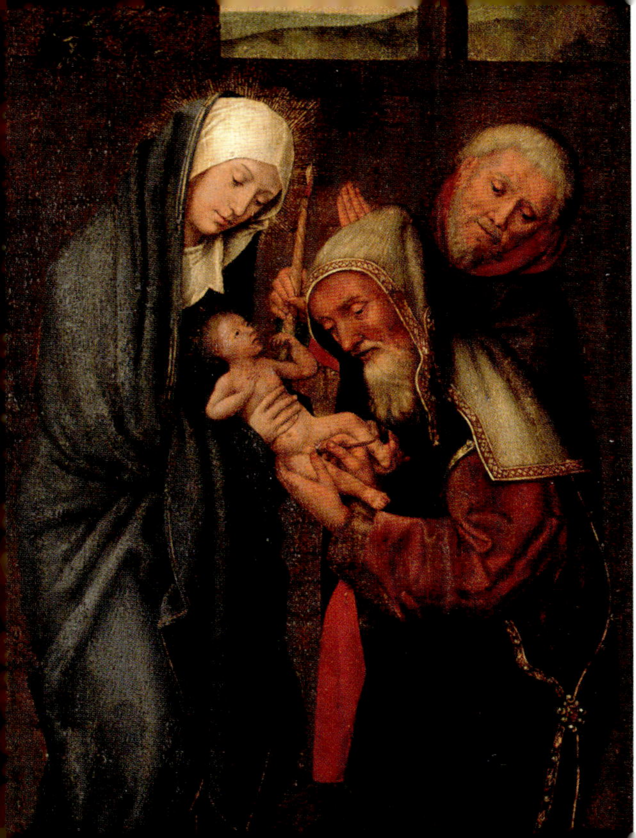

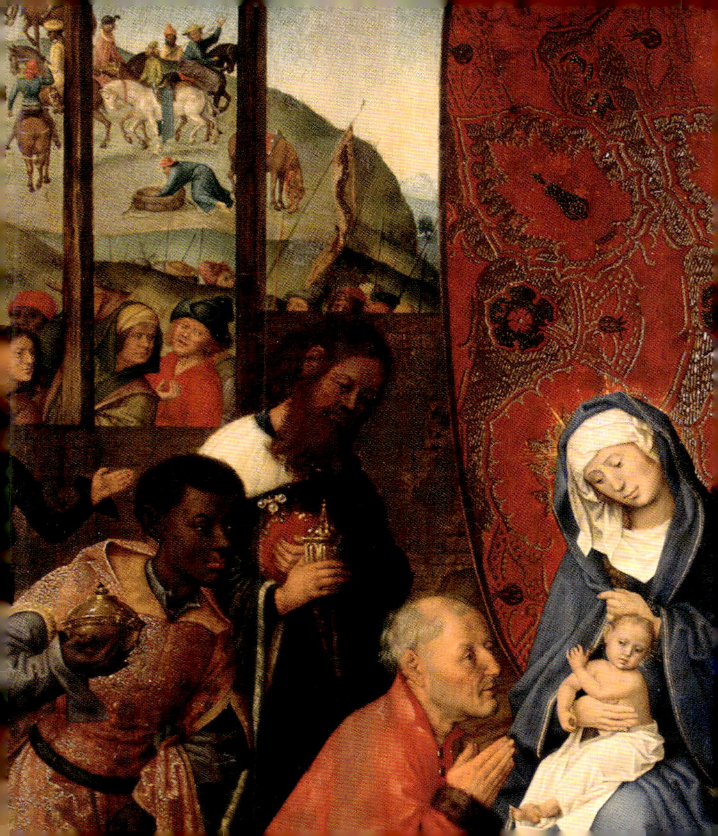

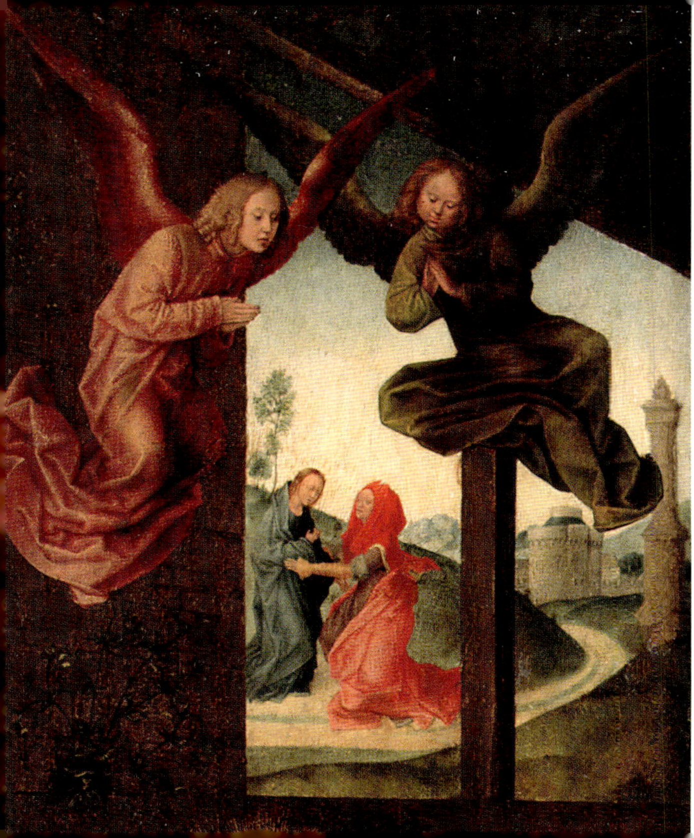

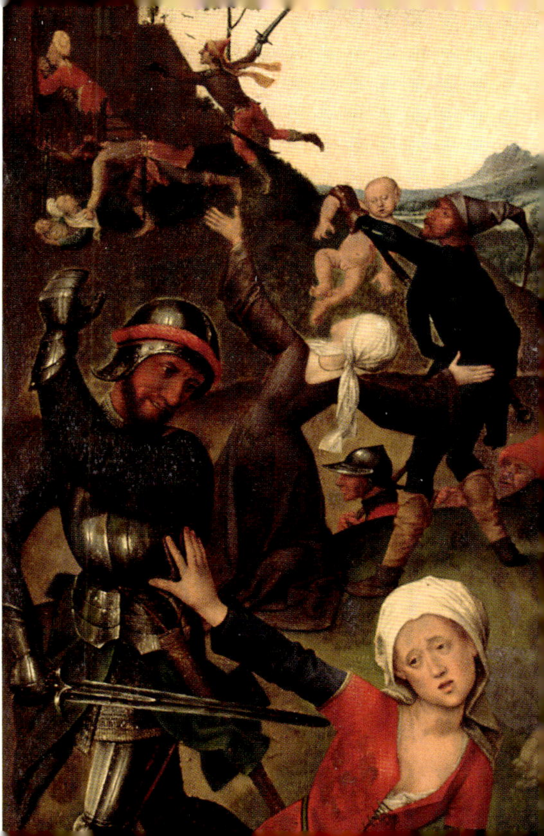

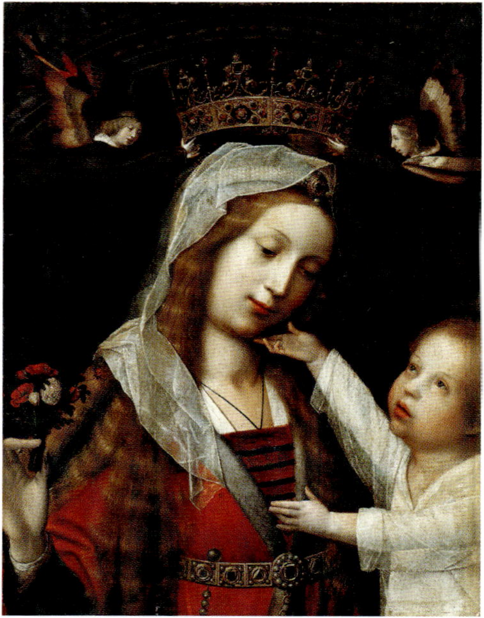

Jan Provost
The Virgin and Child
Late 15th – early 16th century. Netherlands

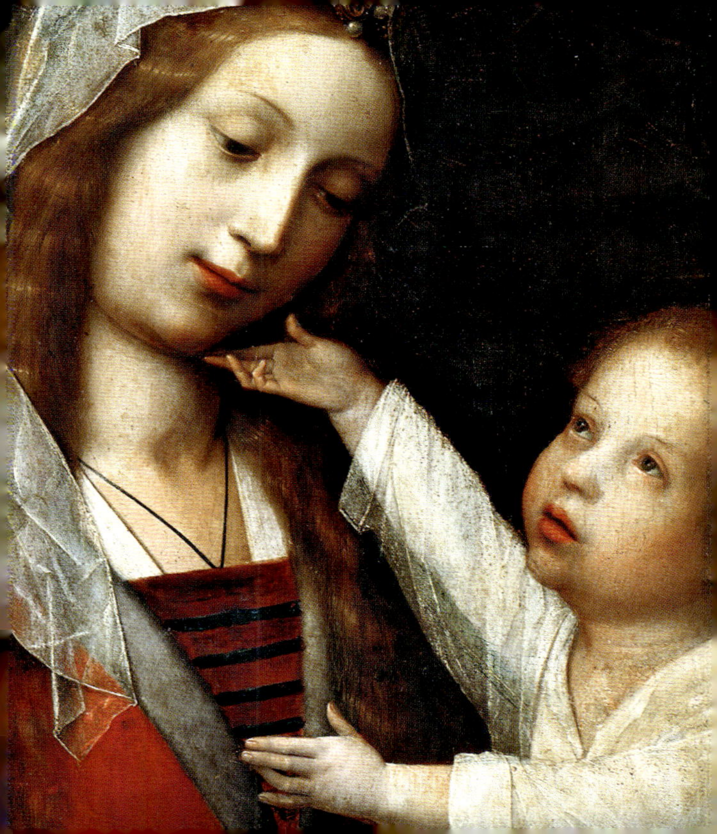

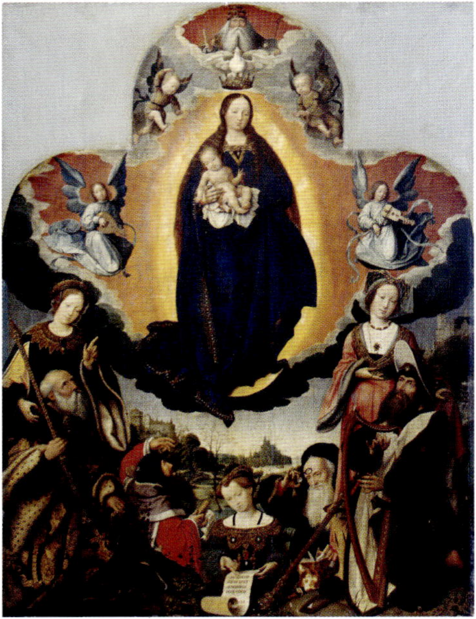

Jan Provost
The Virgin Mary as Queen of Heaven
1524. Netherlands

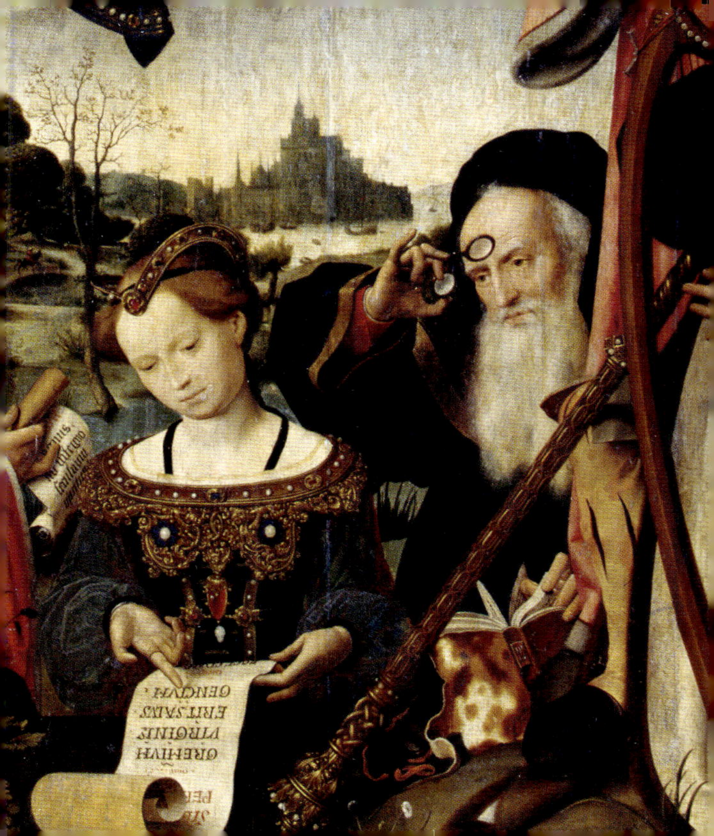

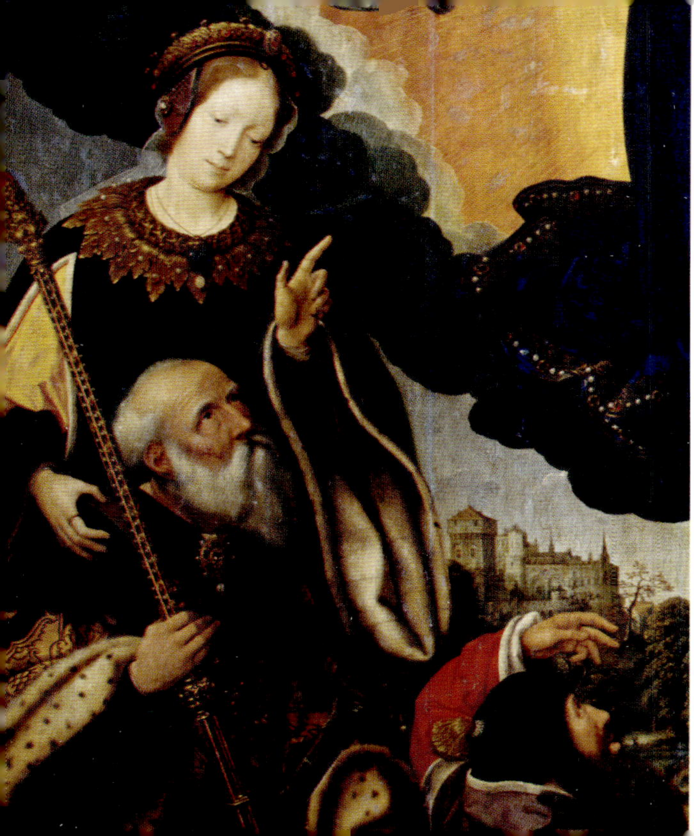

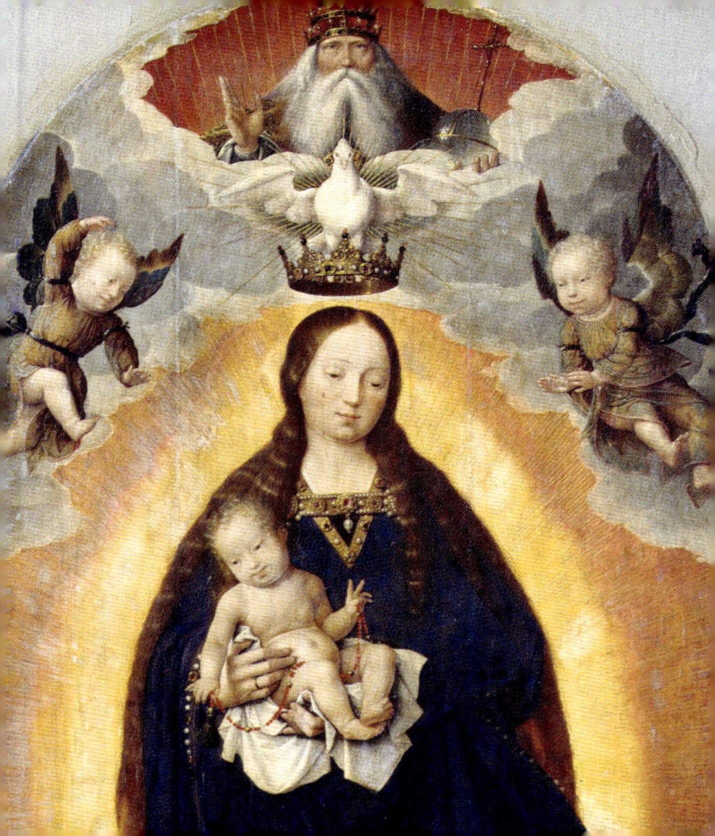

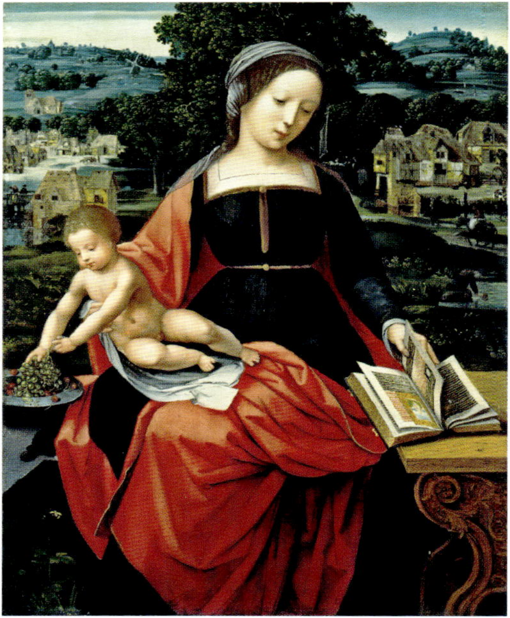

Master of the Female Half-Lengths
The Virgin and Child
First half of the 16th century. Netherlands

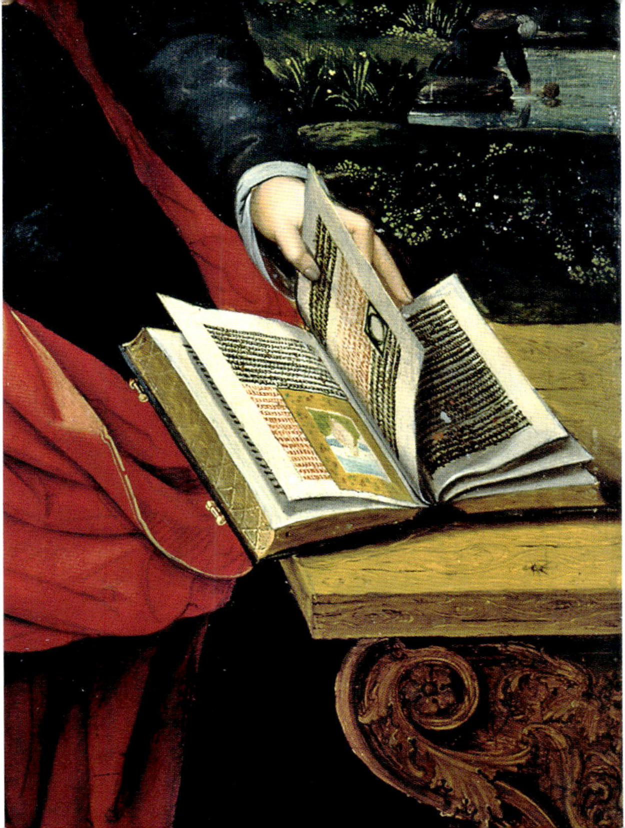

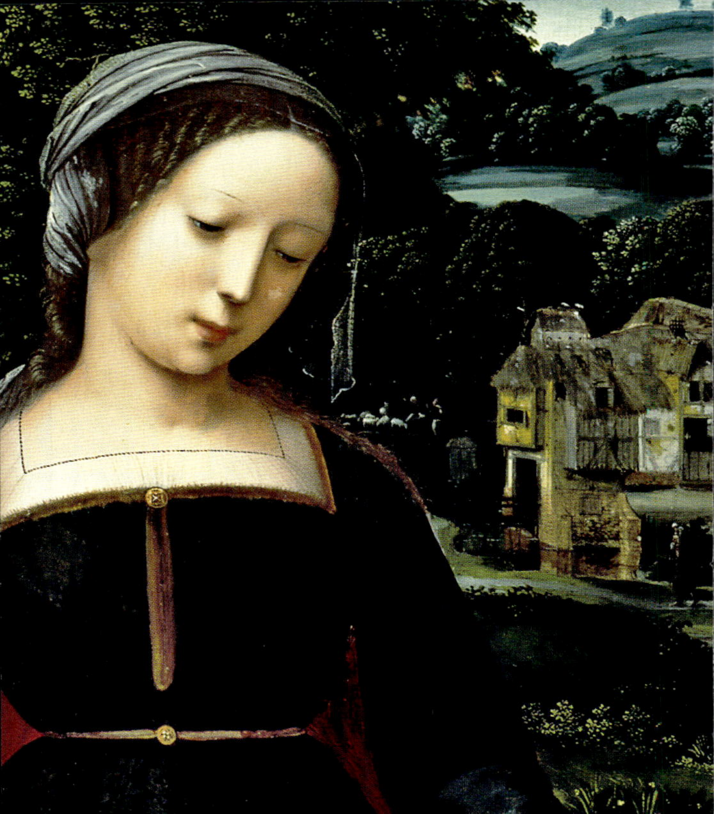

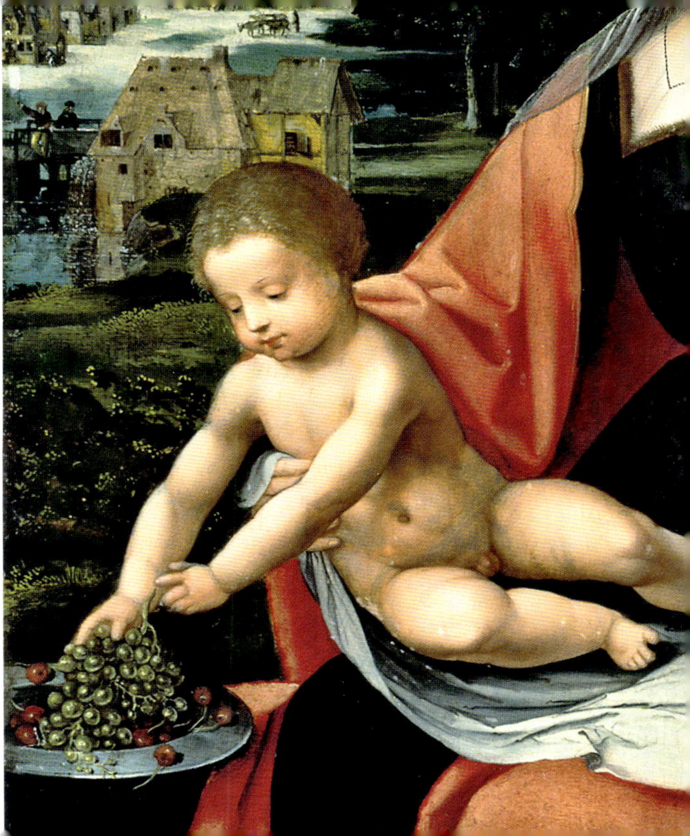

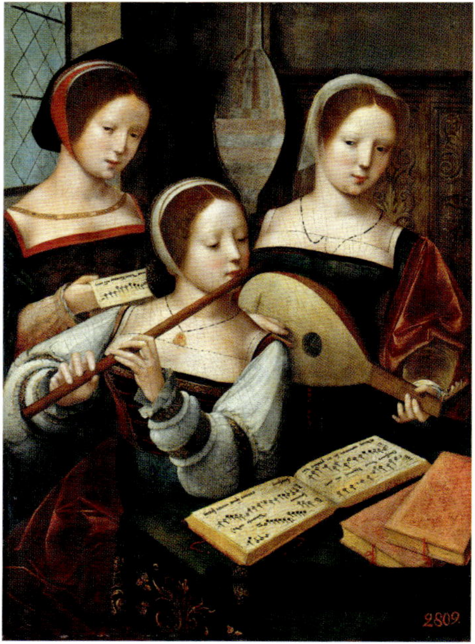

Master of the Female Half-Lengths
Musicians
First half of the 16th century. Netherlands

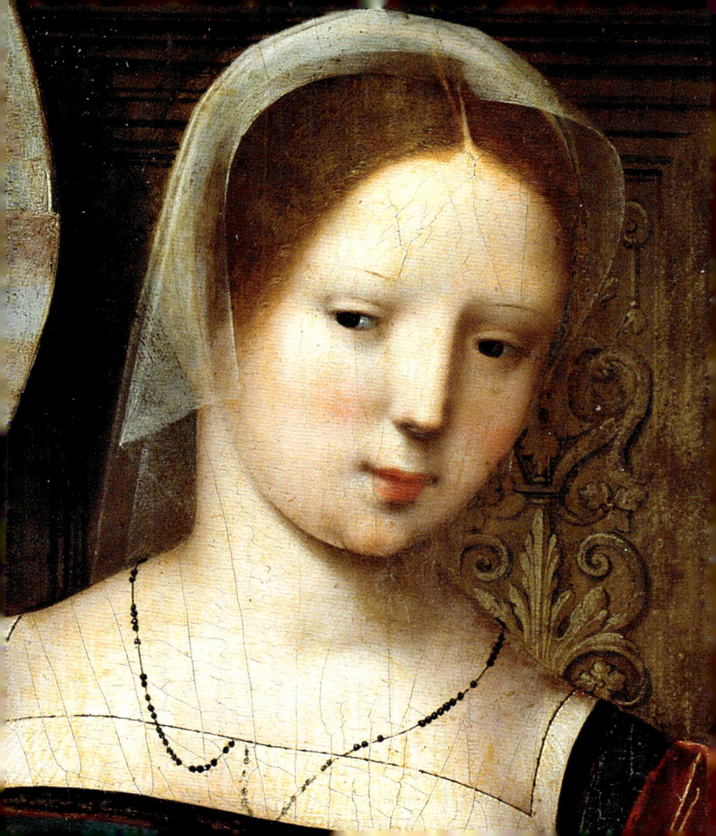

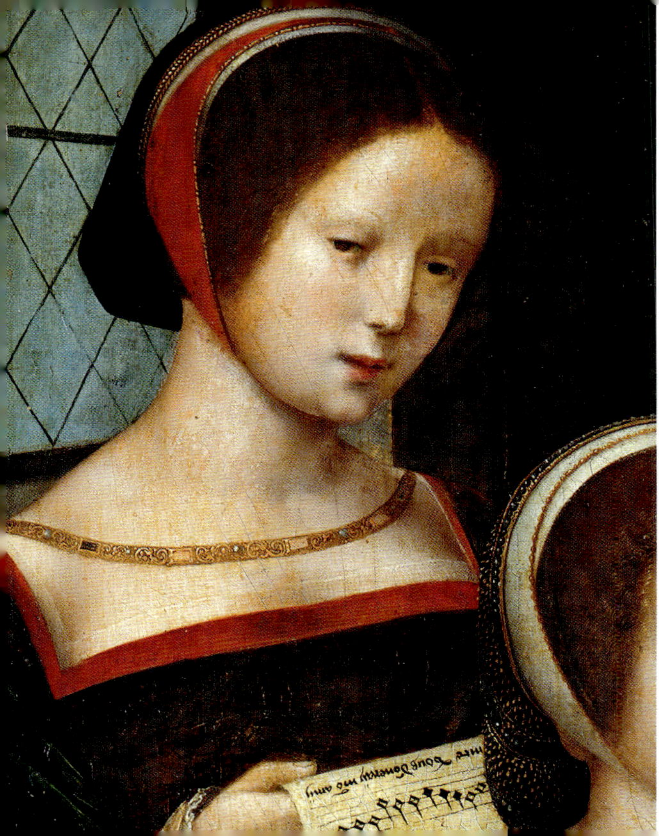

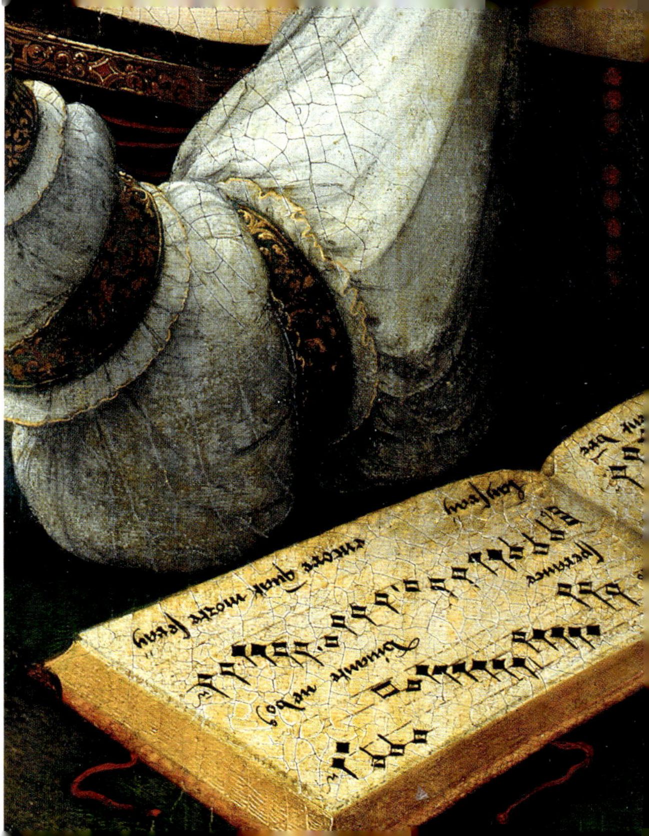
encore quant morte seray

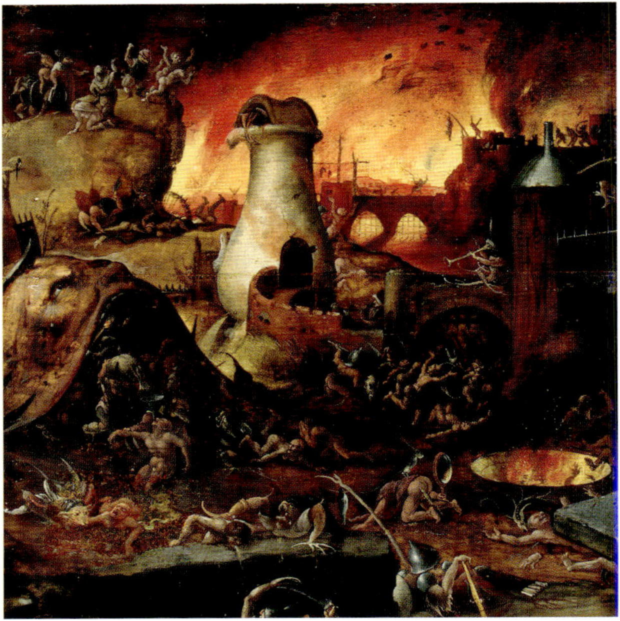

Circle of Hieronymus Bosch
Hell
Early 16th century. Netherlands

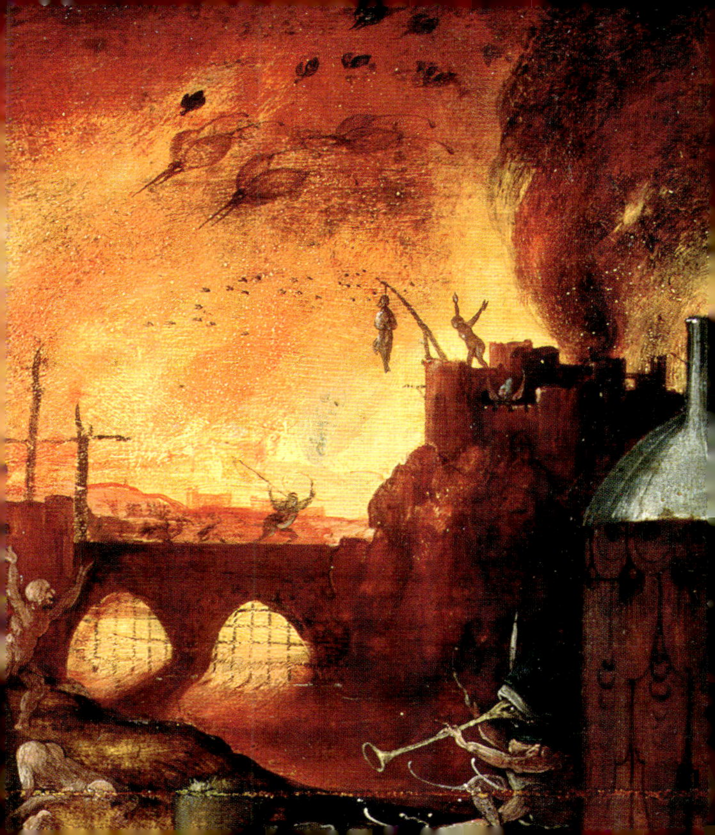

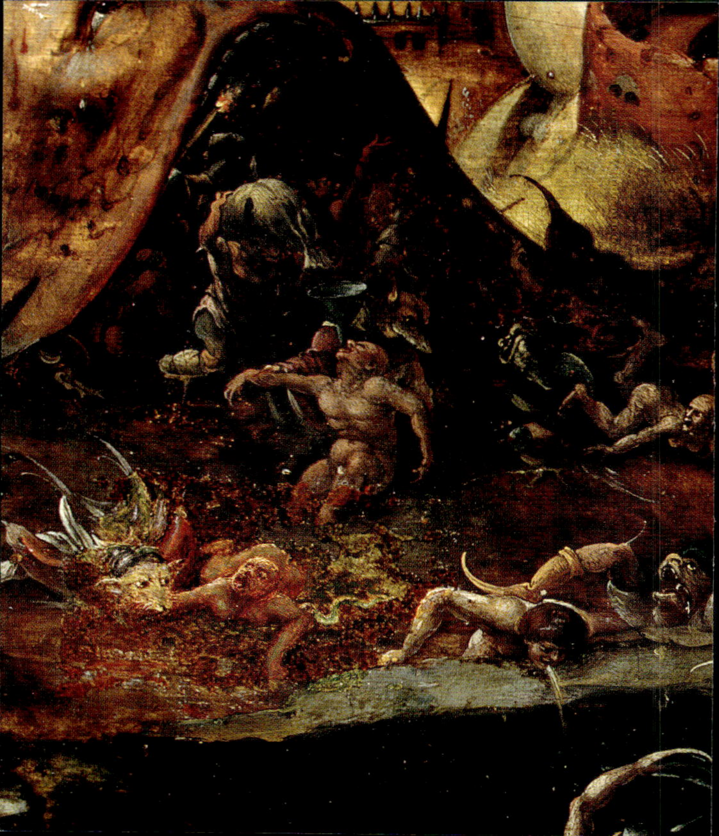

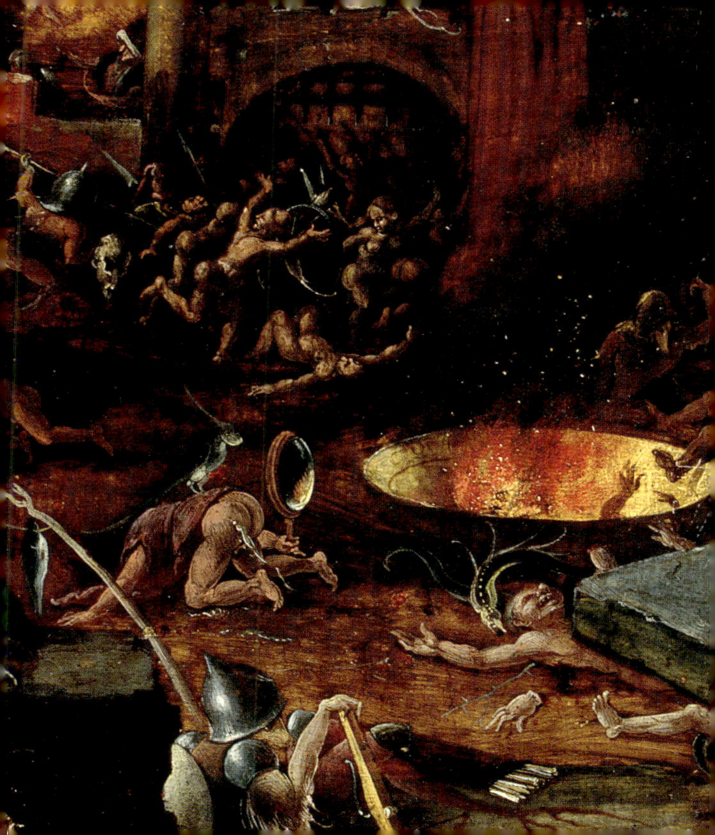

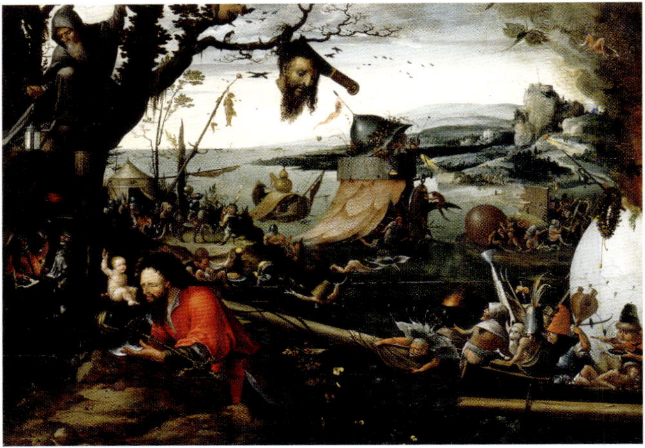

Jan Mandijn
Landscape with the Legend of St Christopher
Early 16th century. Netherlands

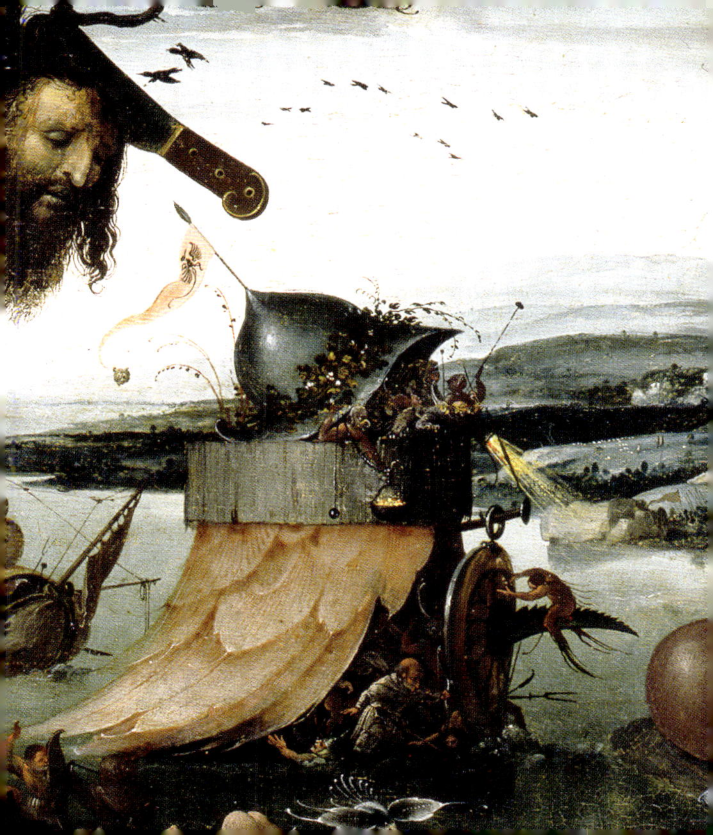

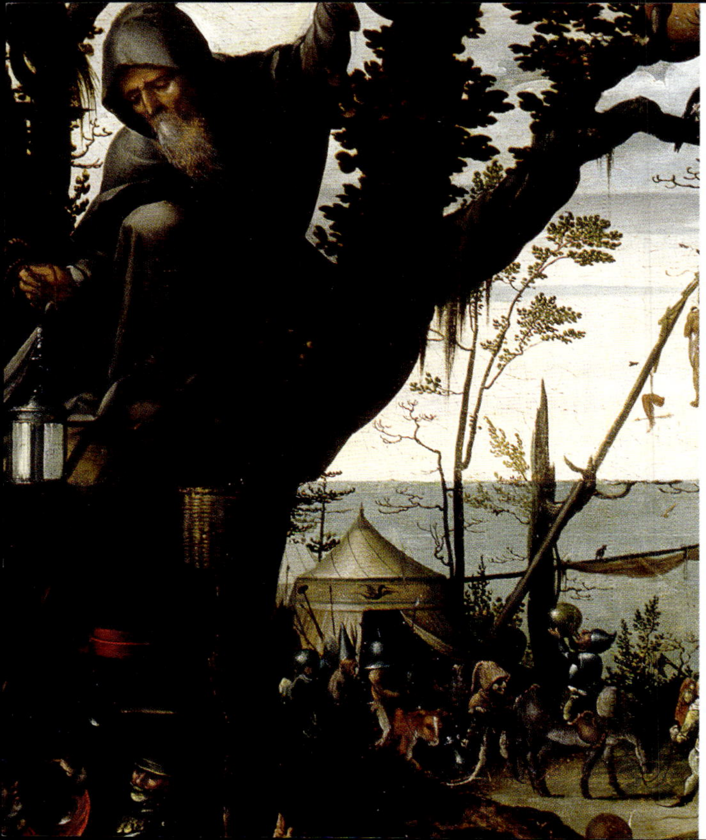

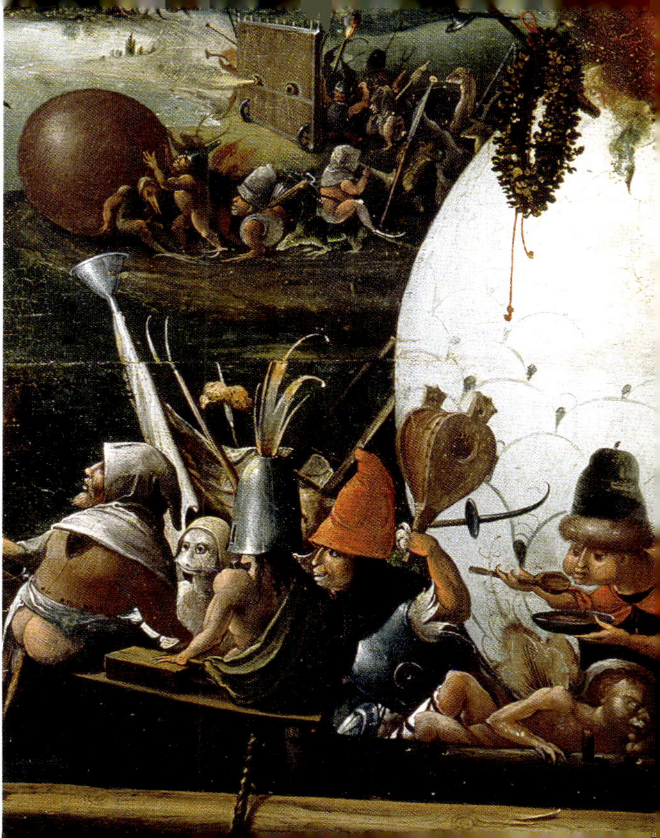

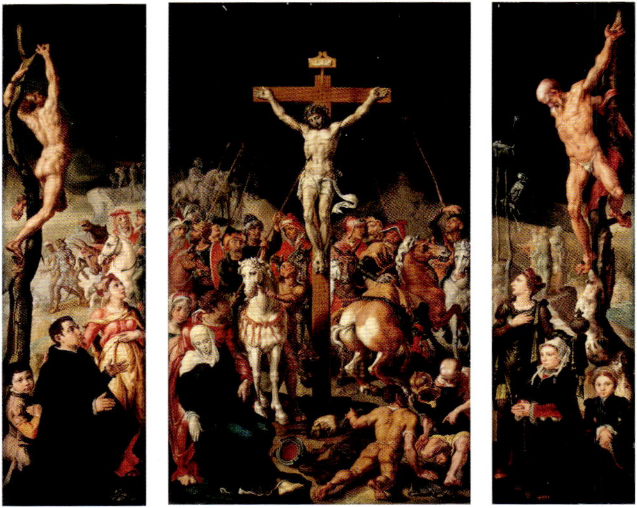

Maarten van Heemskerck
Calvary. Triptych
Middle 16th century
Netherlands

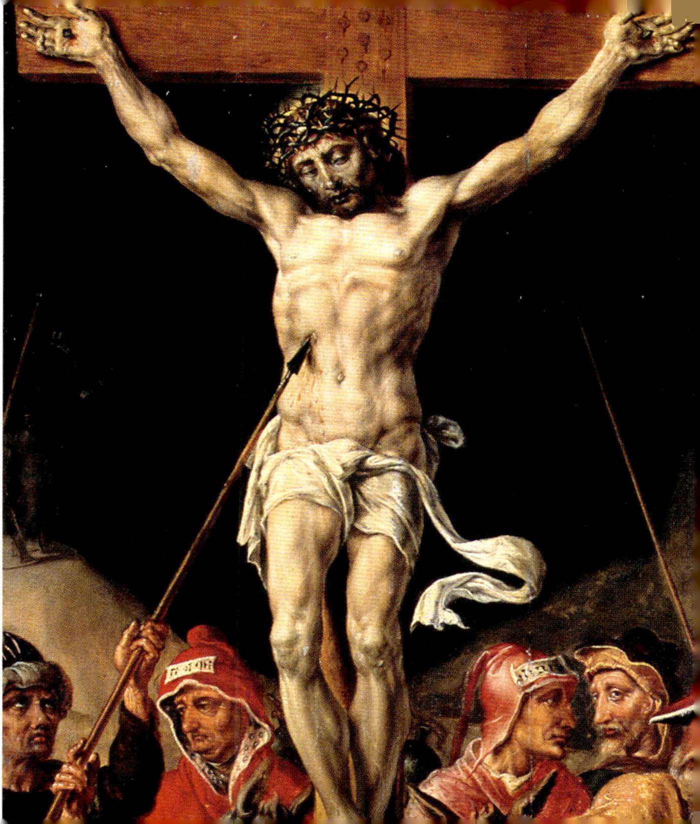

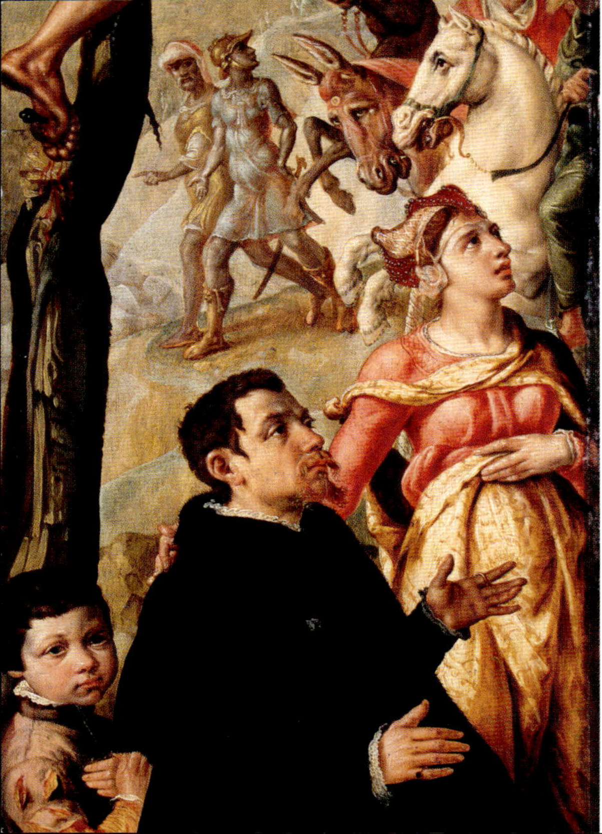

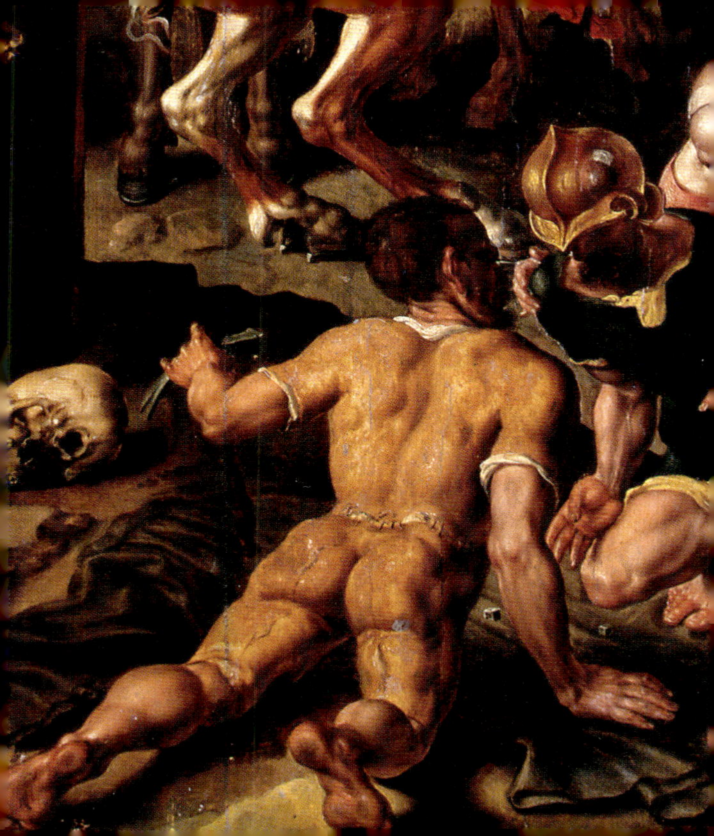

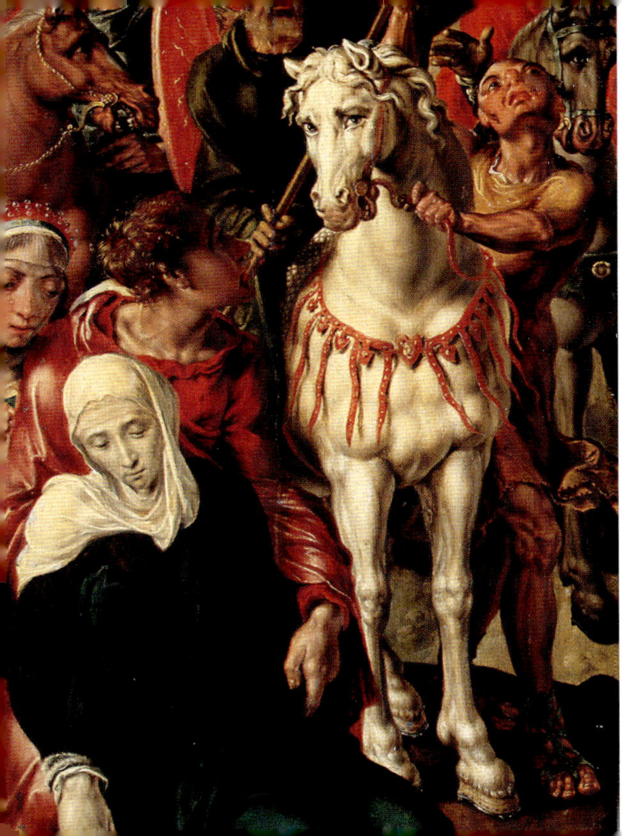

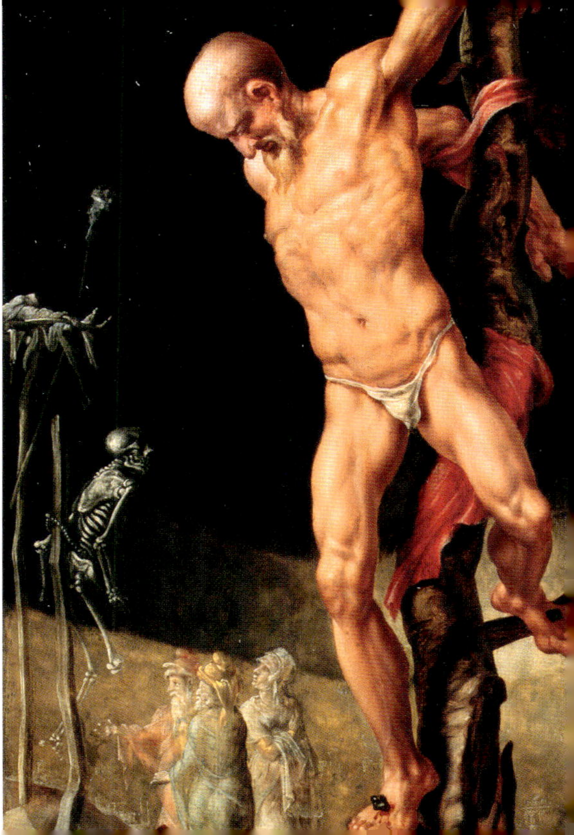

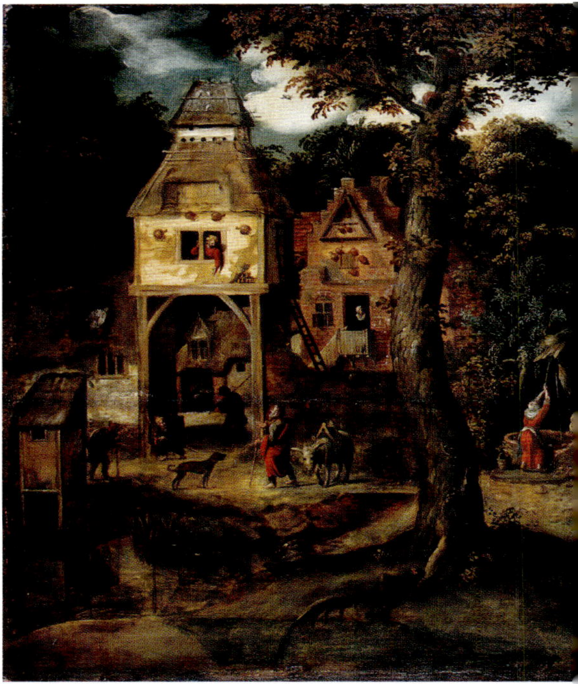

Joachim Patinir
Landscape with the Rest on the Flight into Egypt
Circa 1524 (?). Netherlands

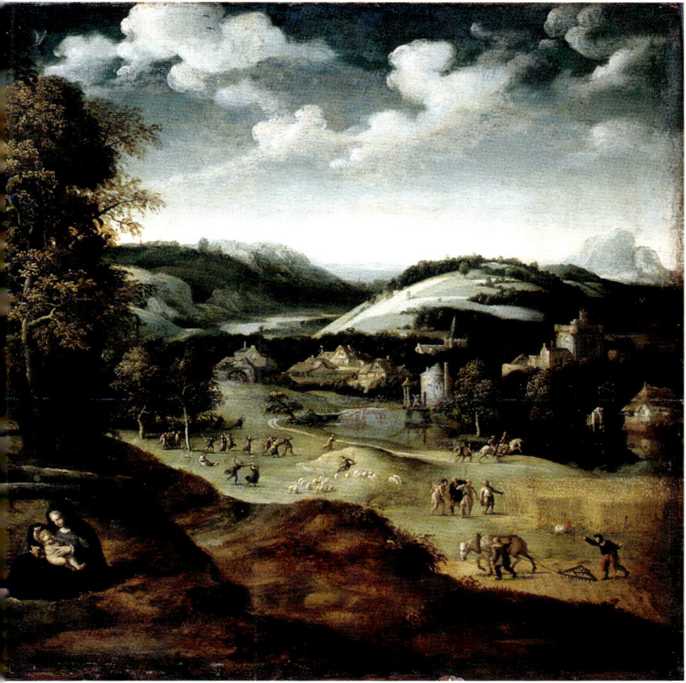

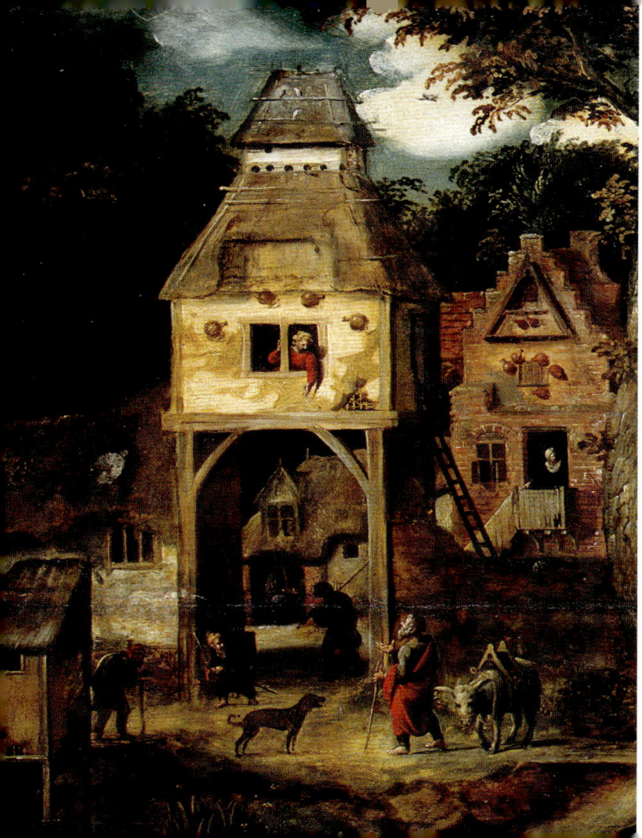

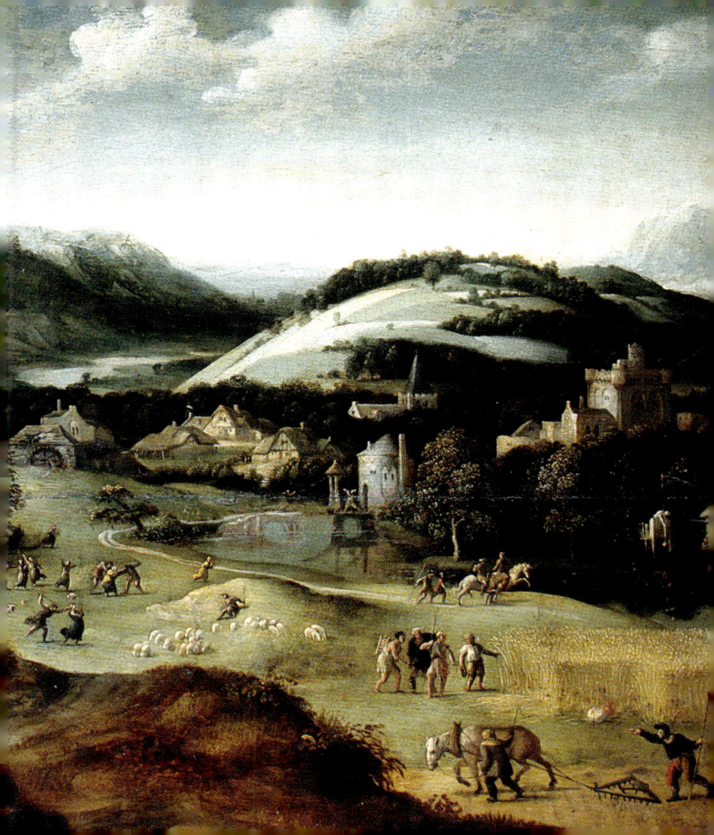

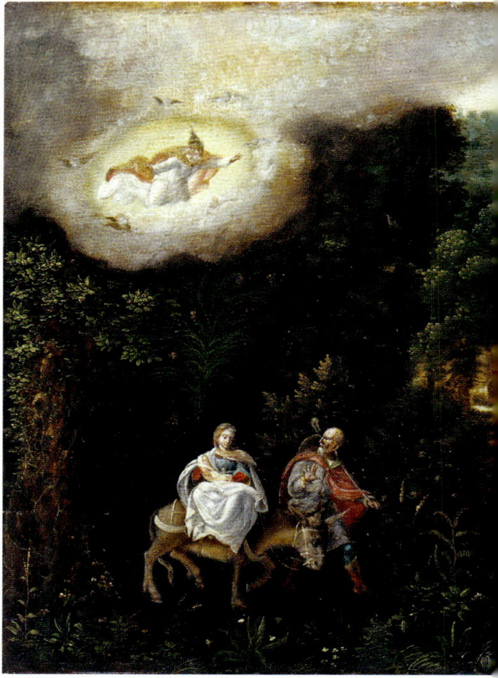

Herri Met de Bles

Landscape with the Flight into Egypt

Early 16th century (?). Netherlands

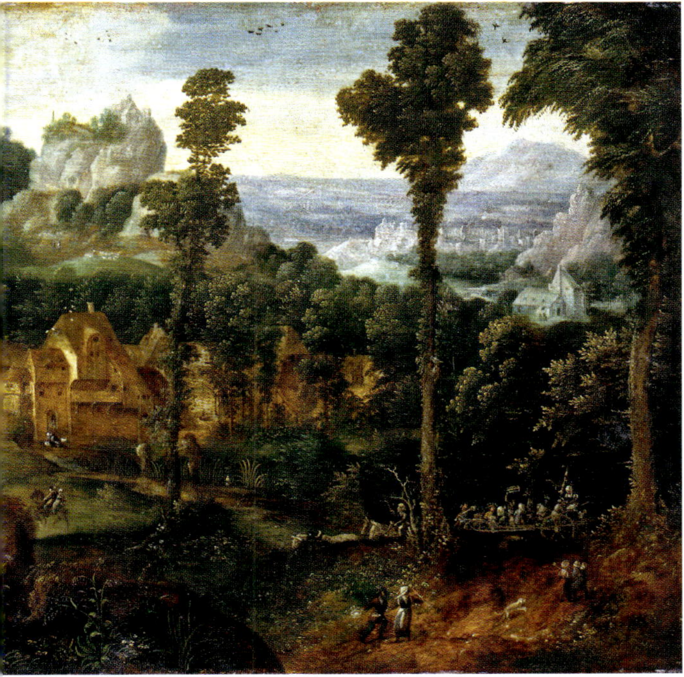

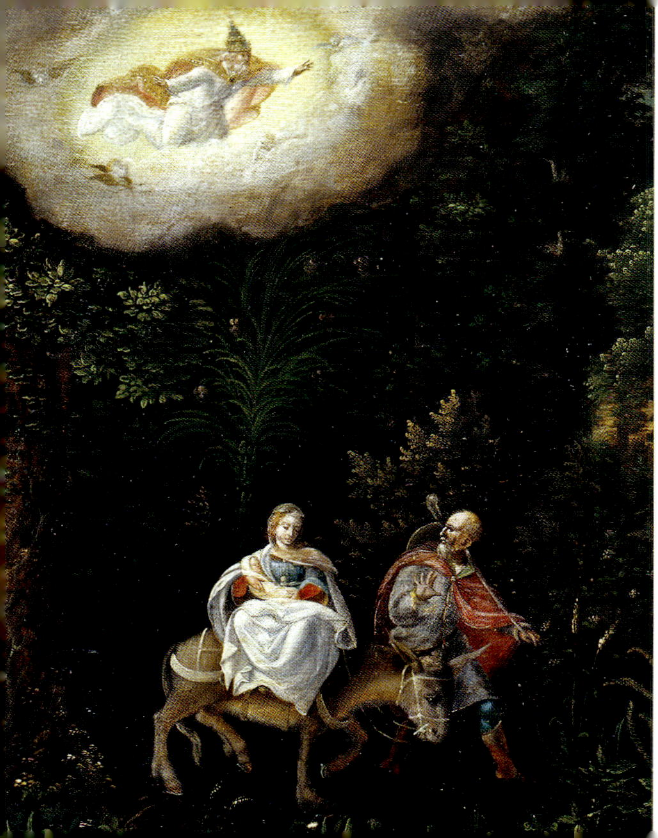

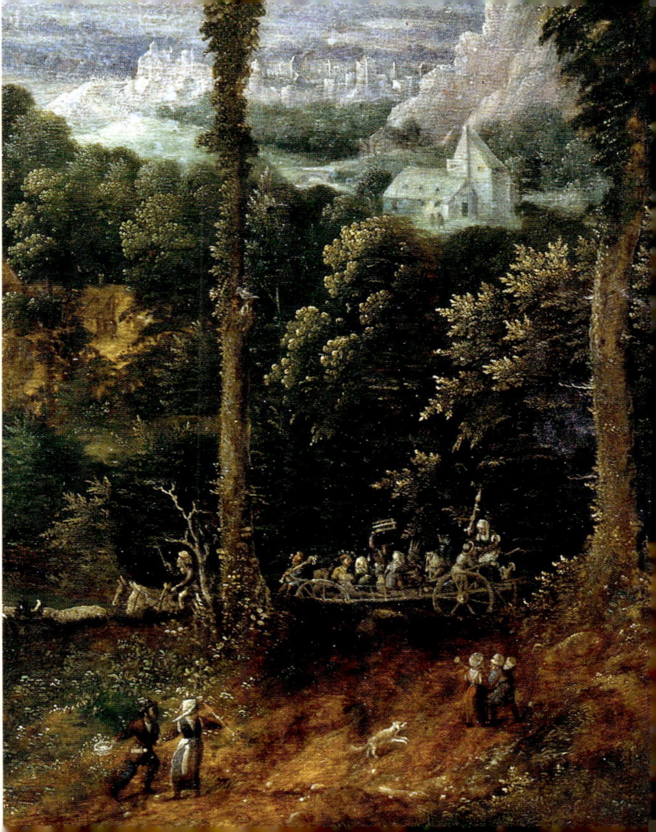

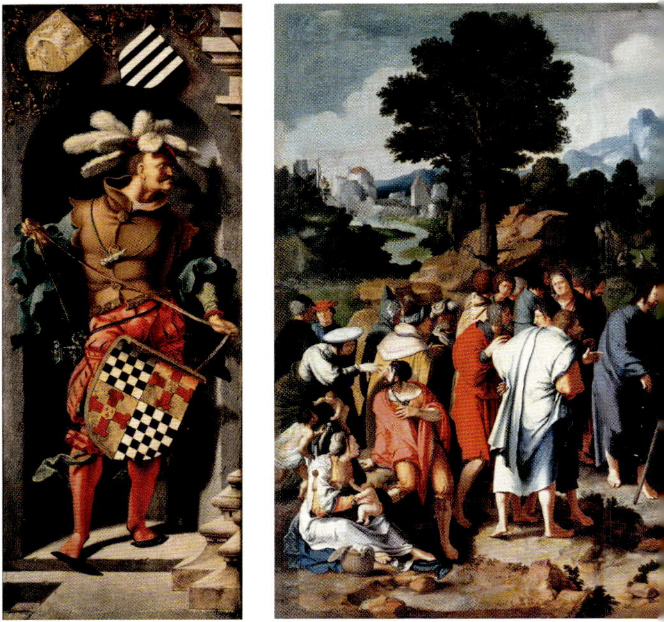

Lucas van Leyden

The Healing of the Blind Man of Jericho. Triptych

1531. Netherlands

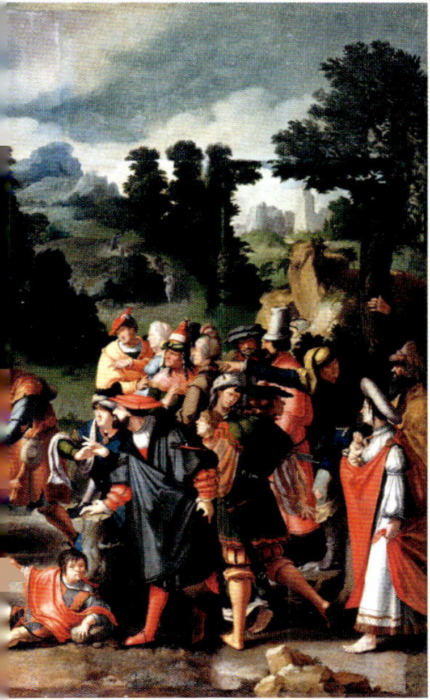

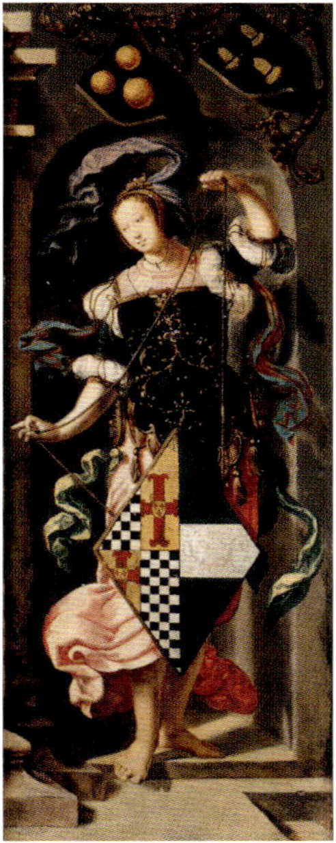

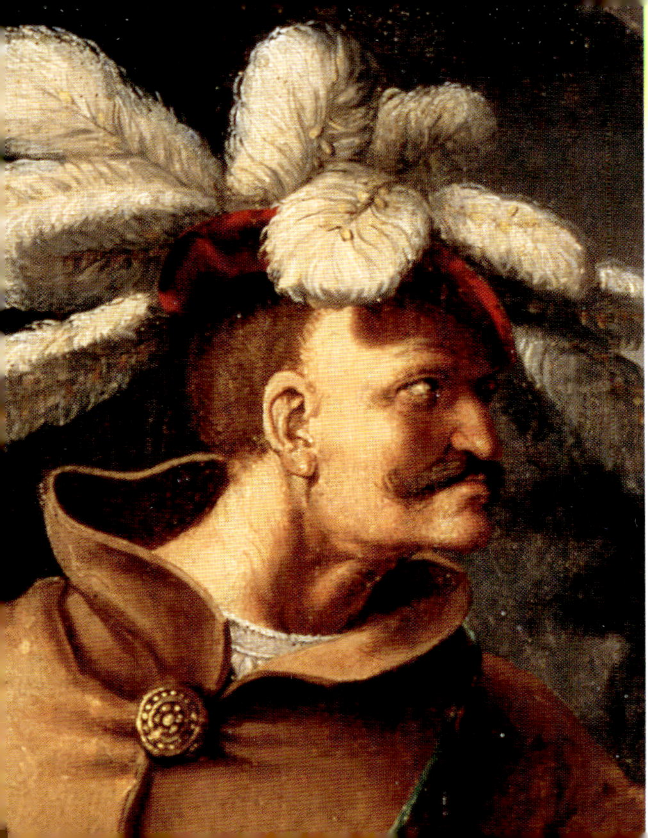

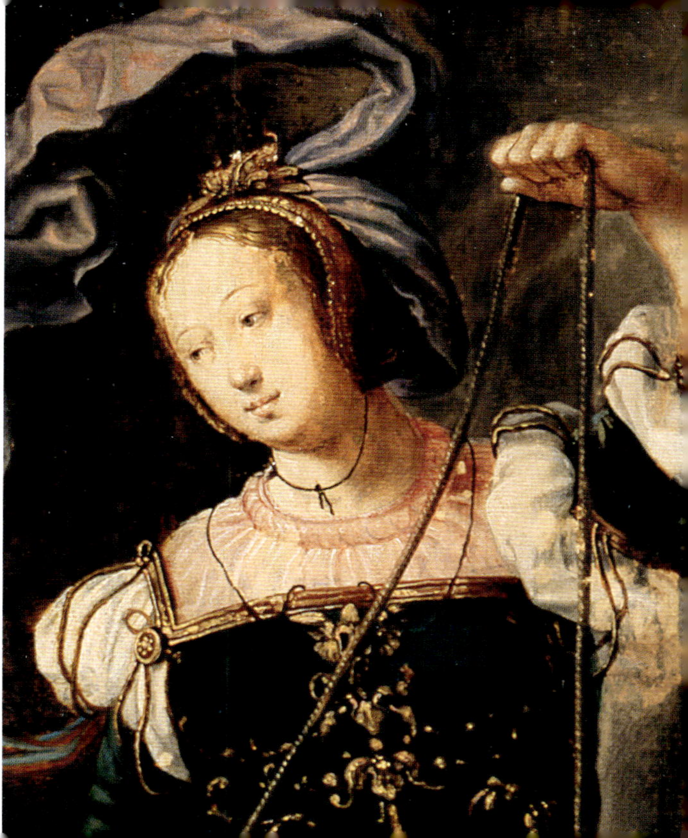

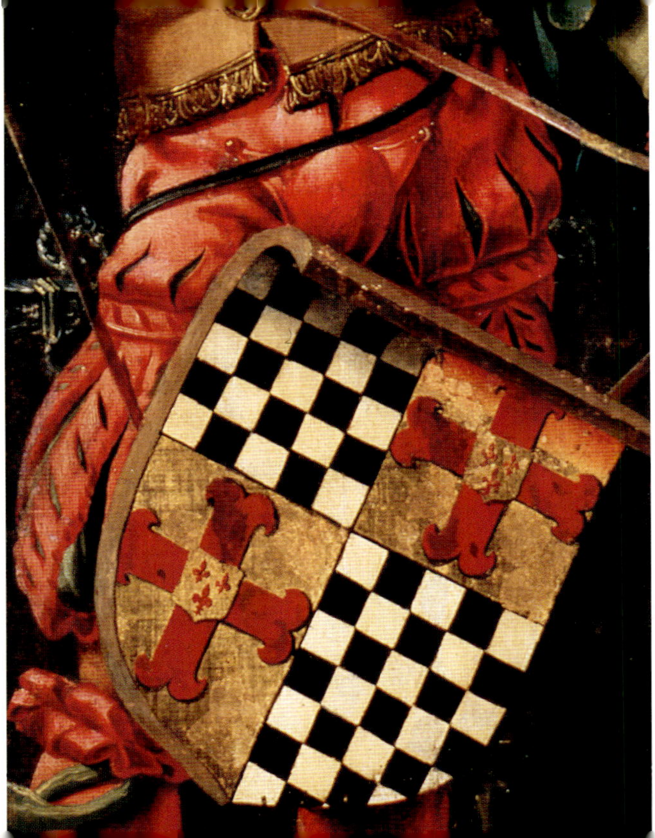

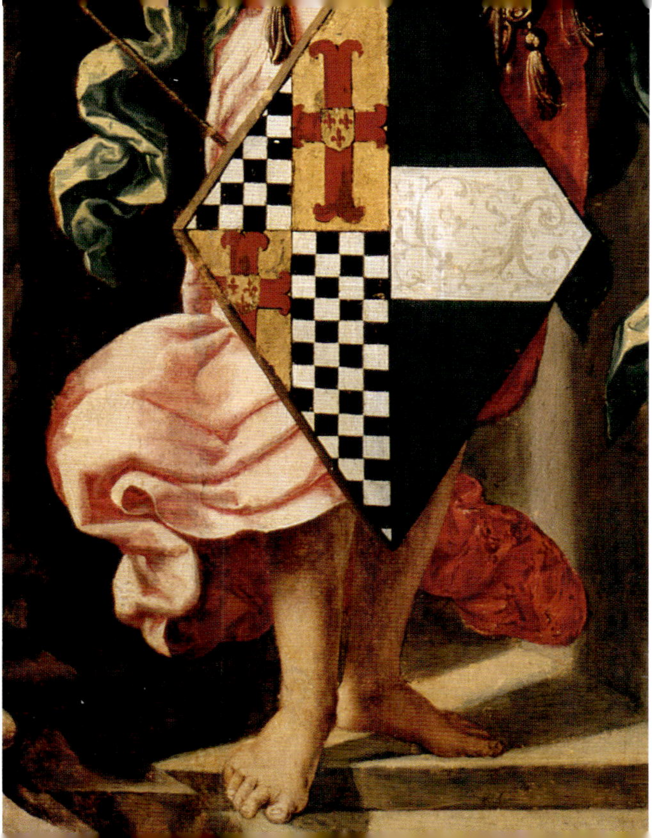

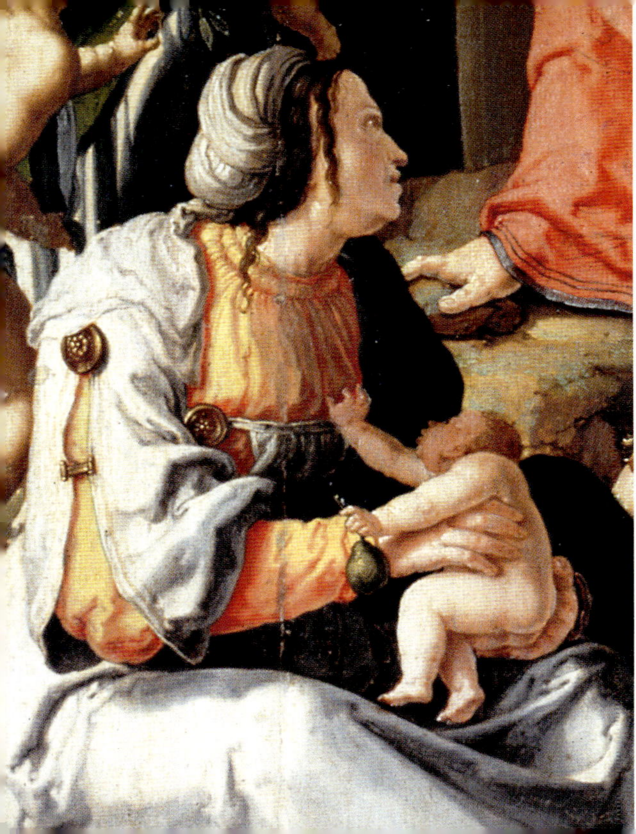

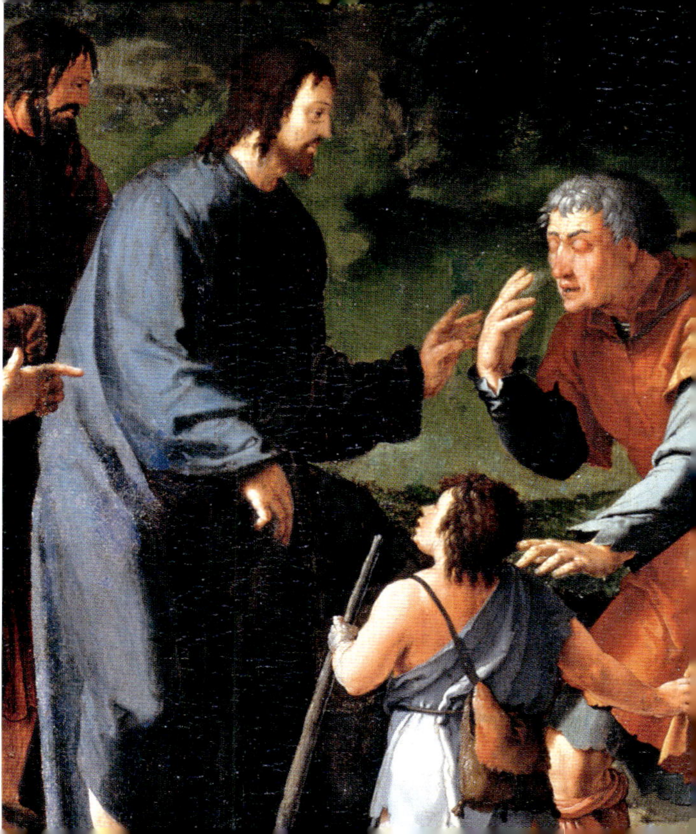

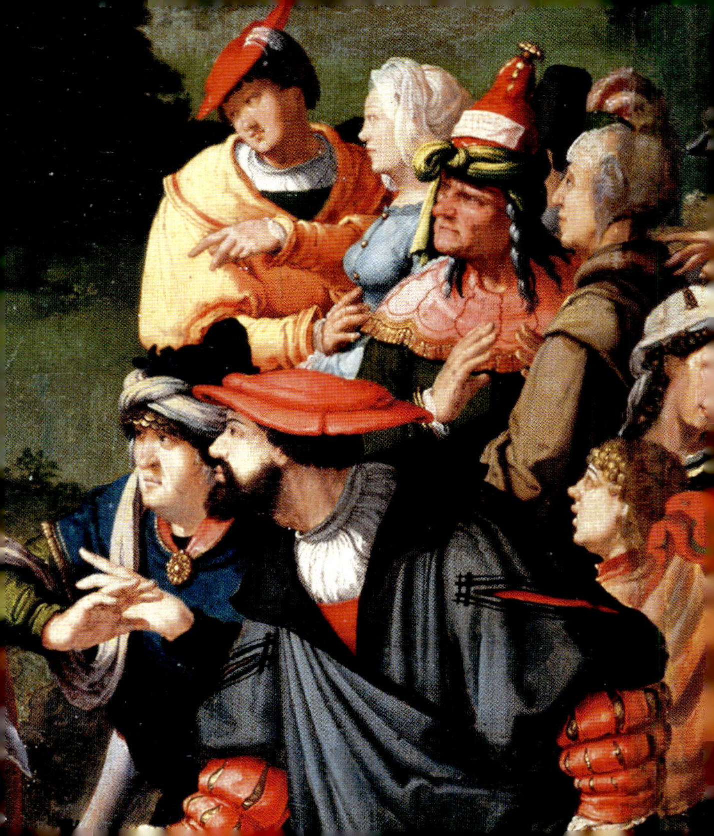

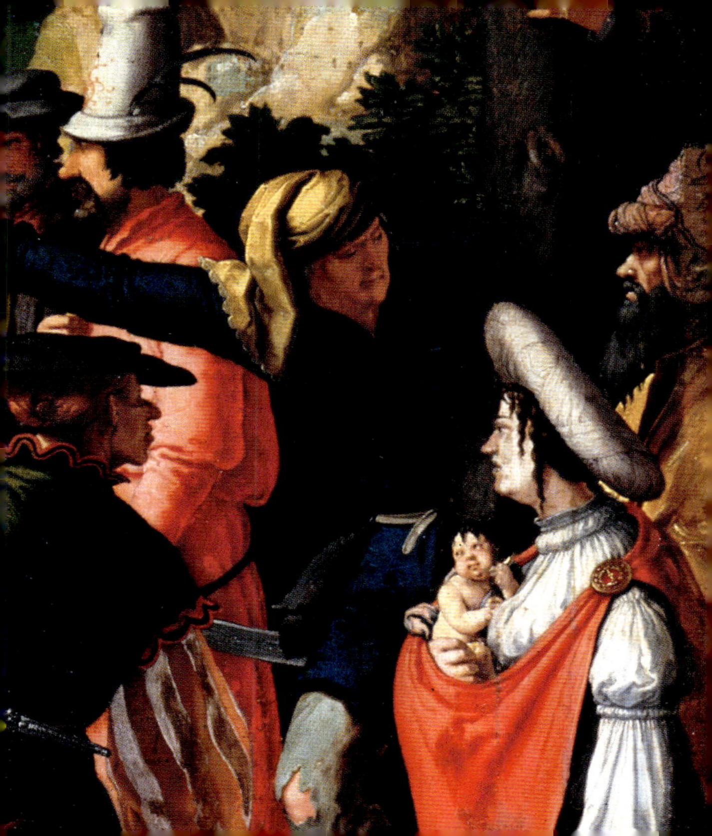

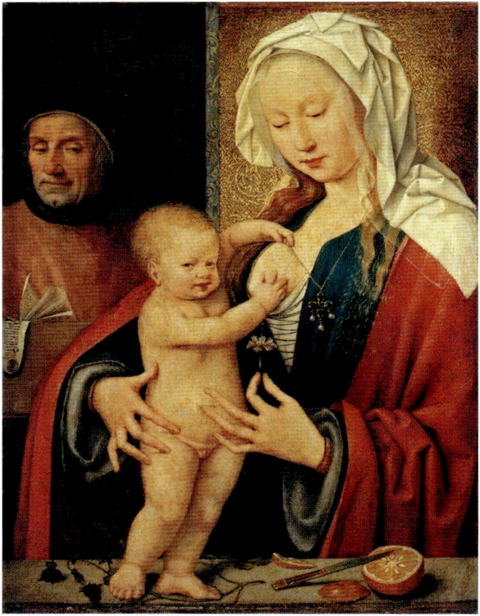

Joos van Cleve
The Holy Family
Late 15th – early 16th century. Netherlands

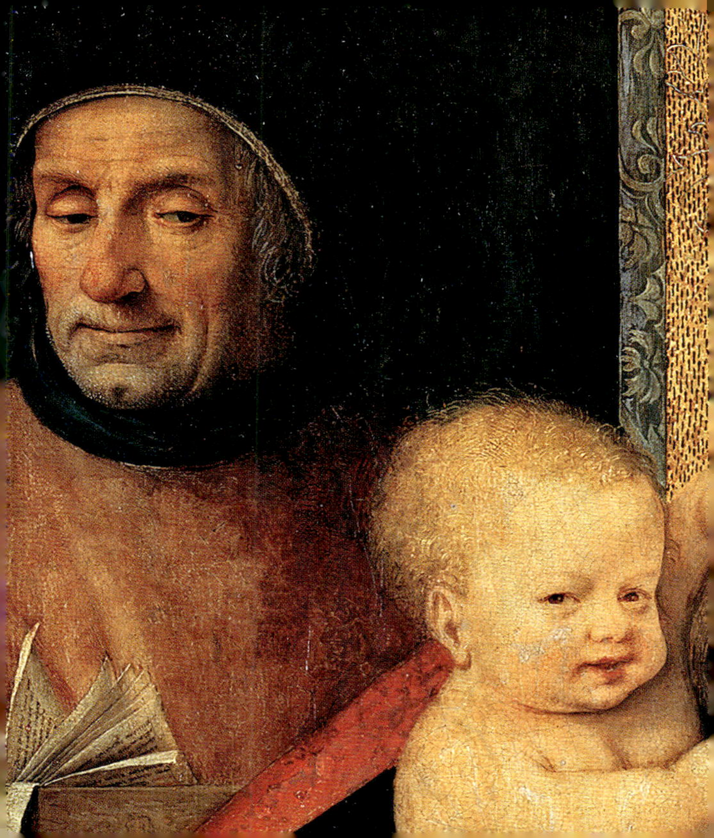

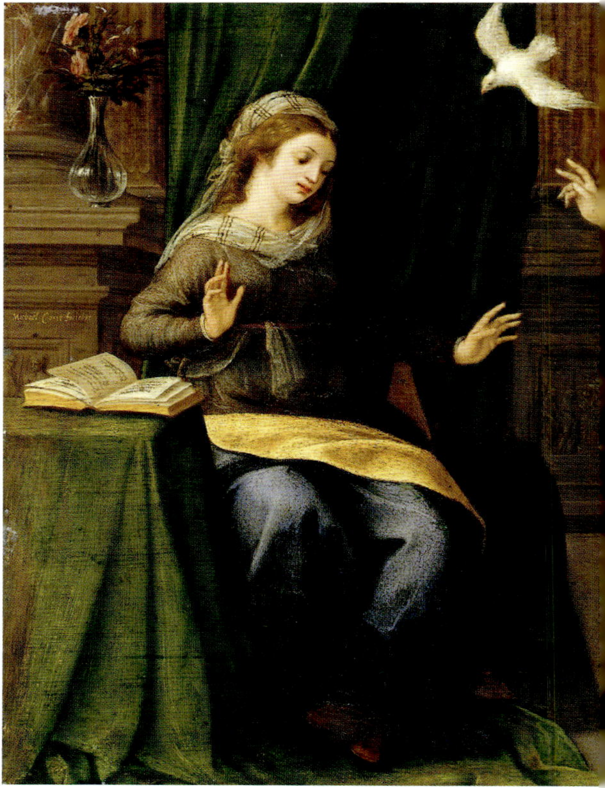

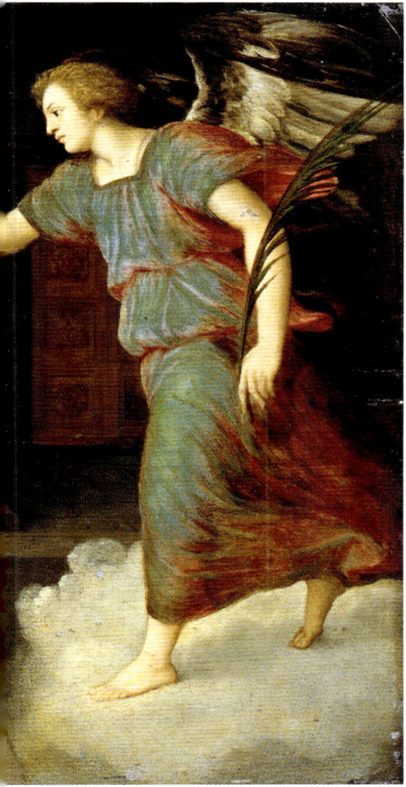

Michiel van Coxie
The Annunciation
Second half of the 16th century
Netherlands

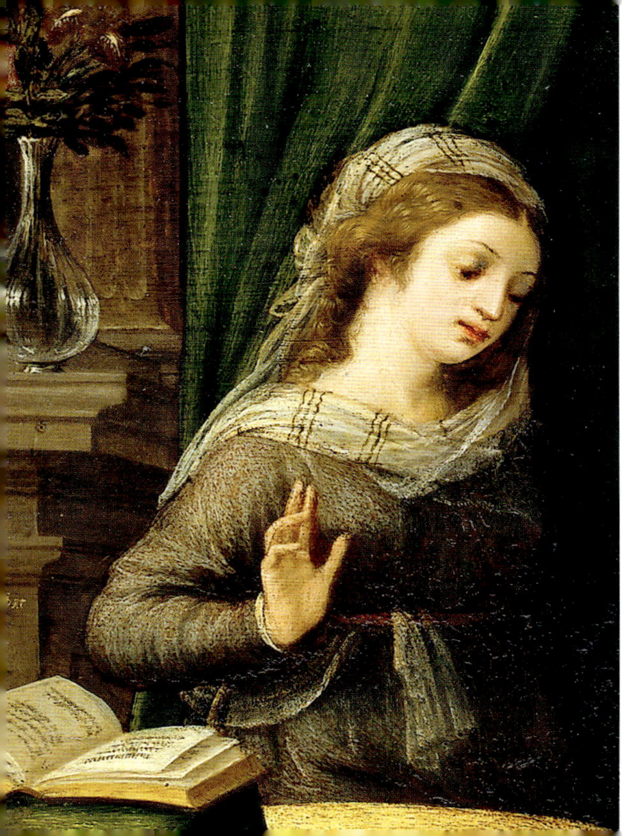

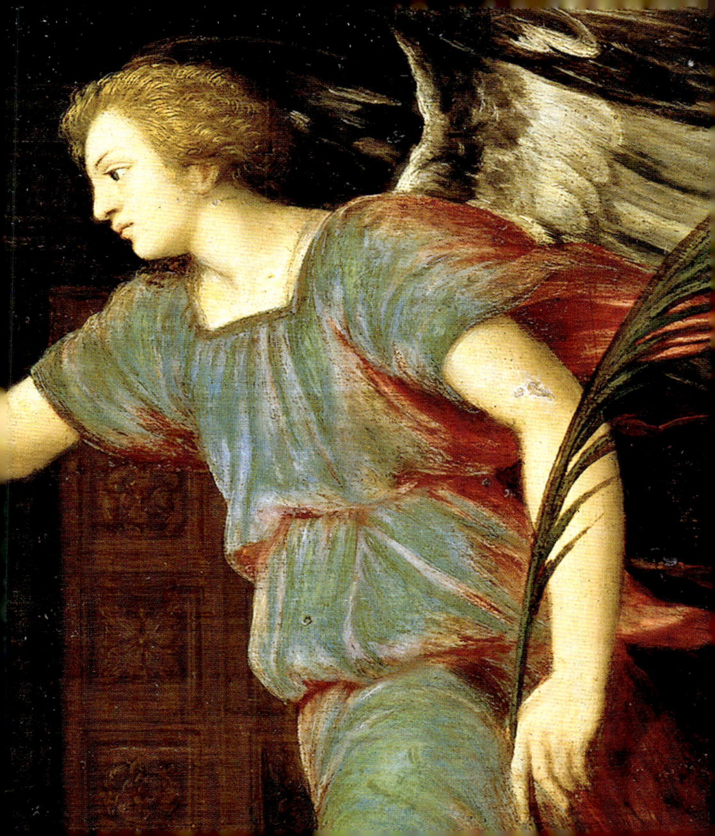

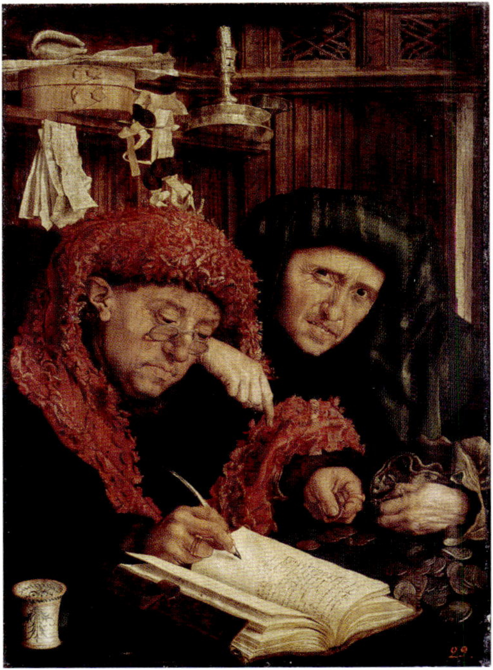

Roemerswaele
The Tax Collectors
16th century
Netherlands

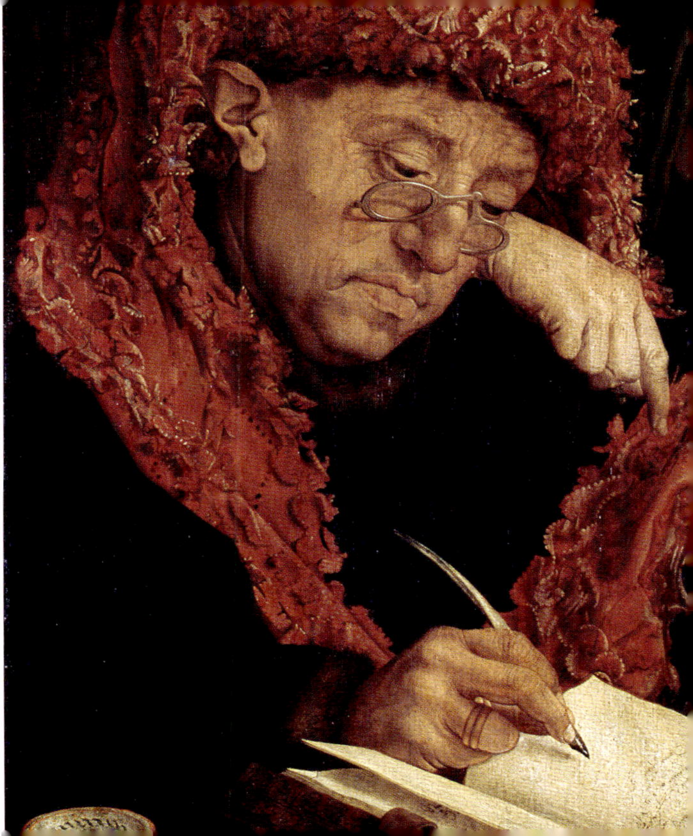

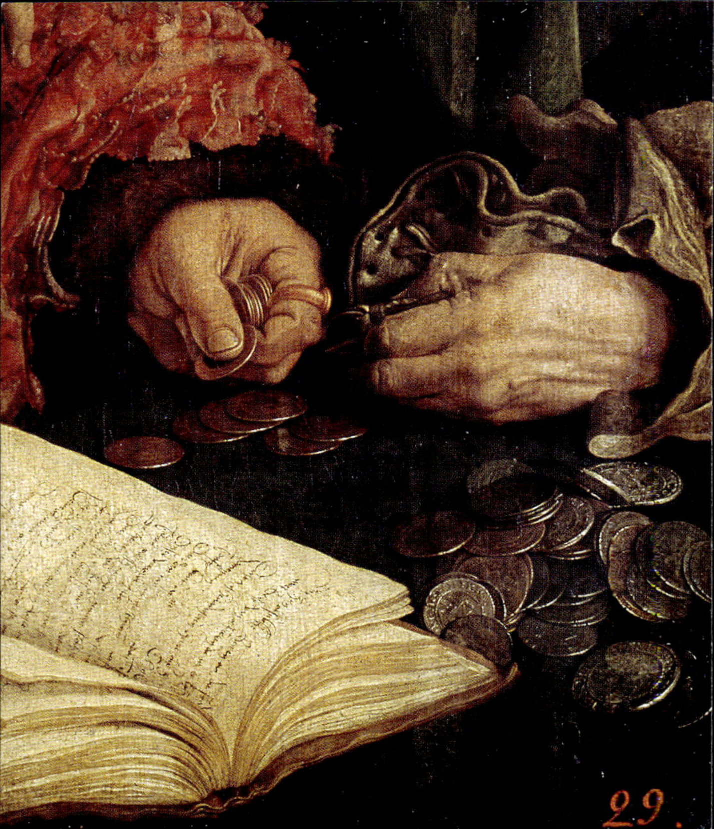

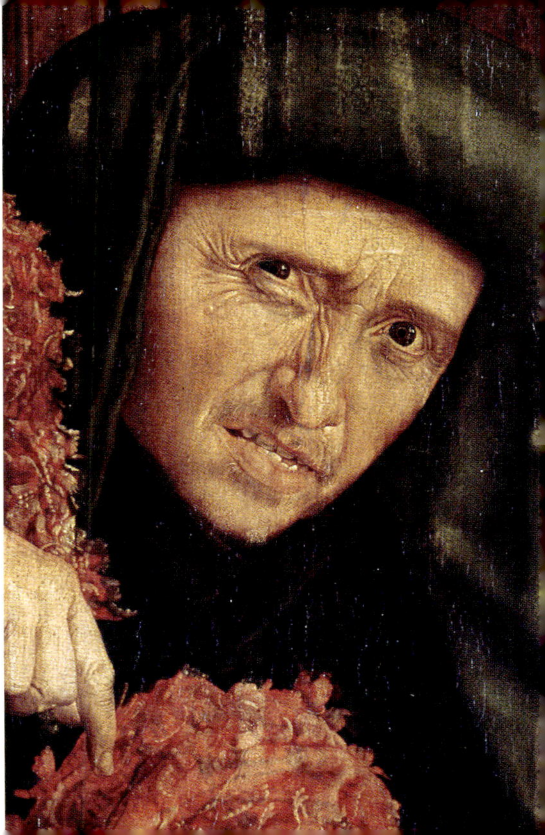

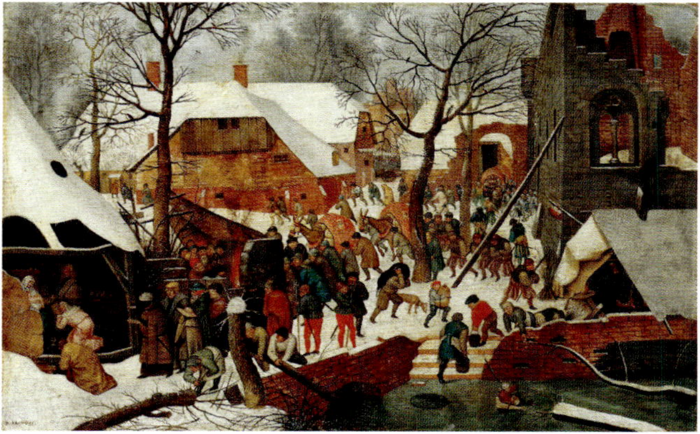

Pieter Brueghel the Younger
The Adoration of the Magi
Second half of the 16th century. Netherlands

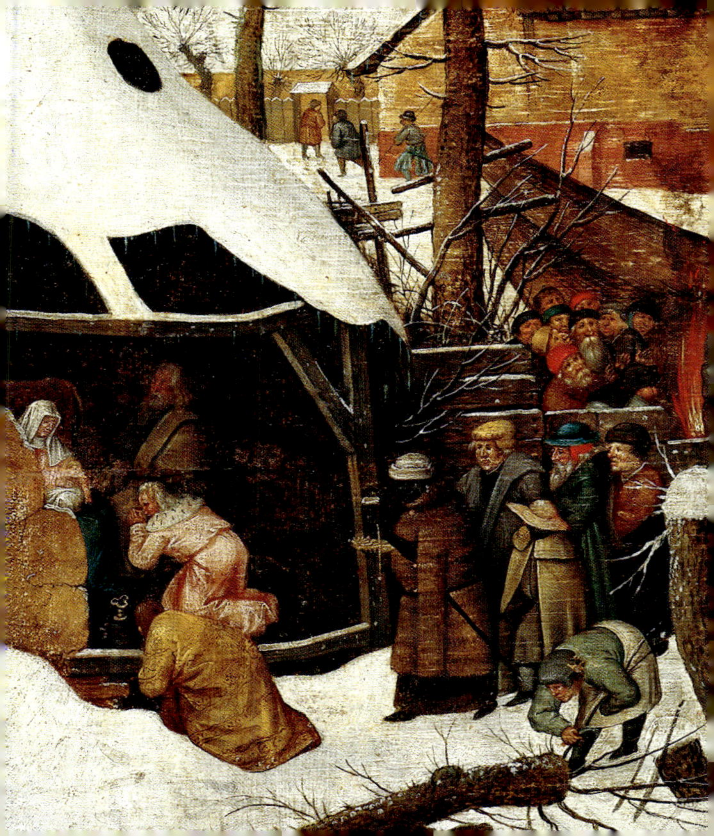

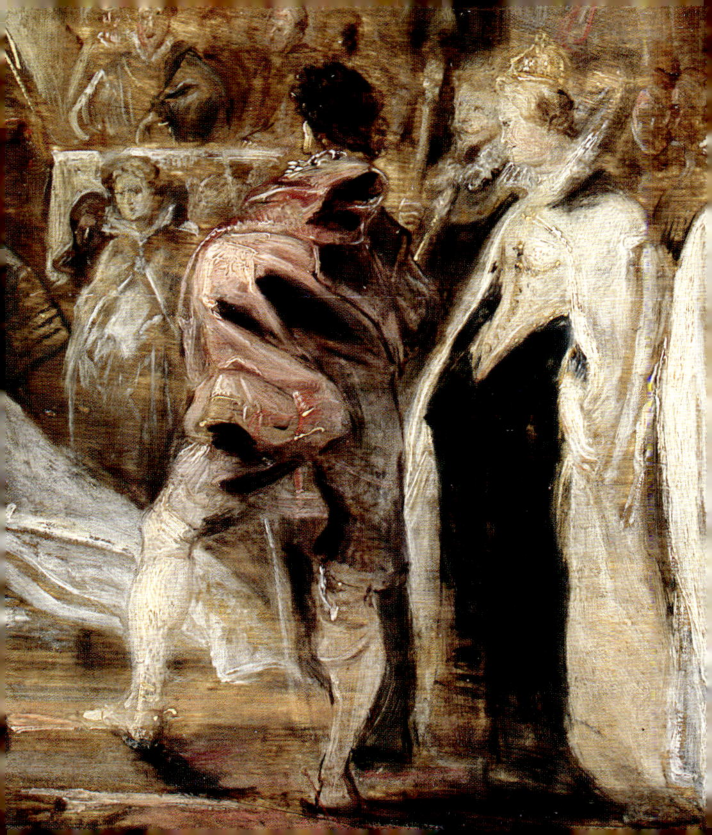

flanders

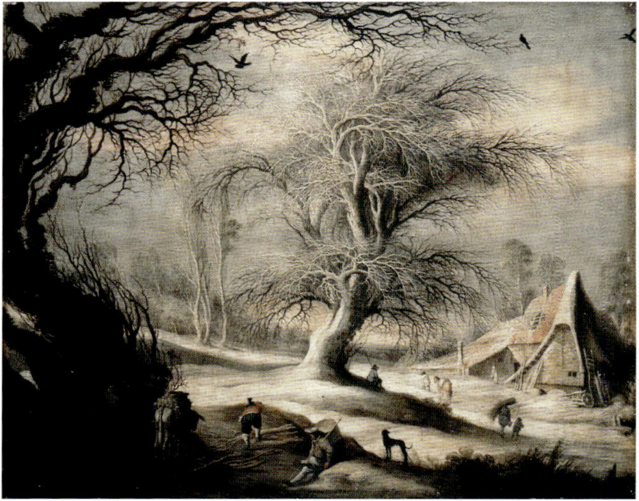

Master of the Winter Landscape (Gijsbrecht Lijtens ?)
Winter Landscape
Late 16th – early 17th century. Flanders

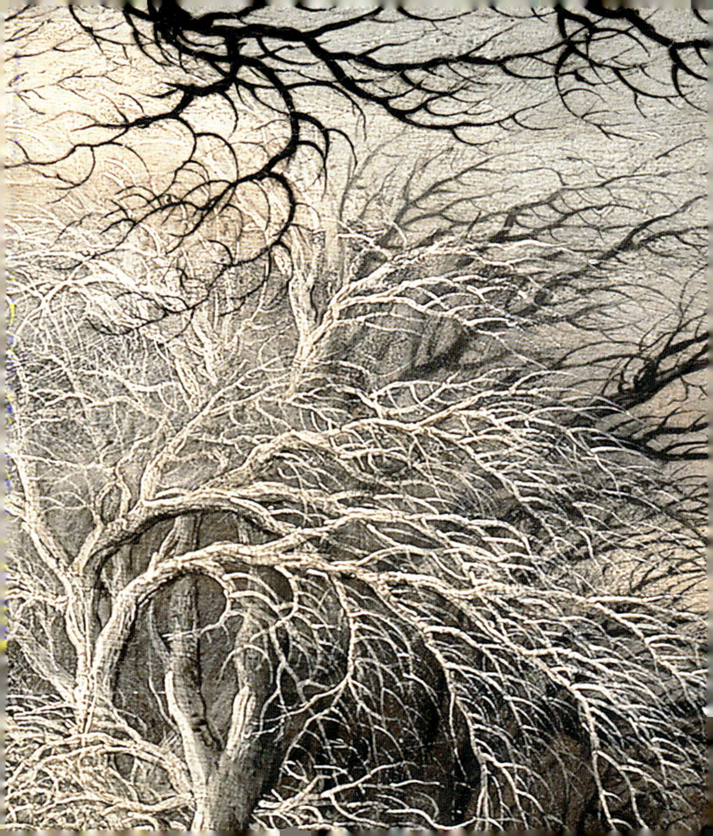

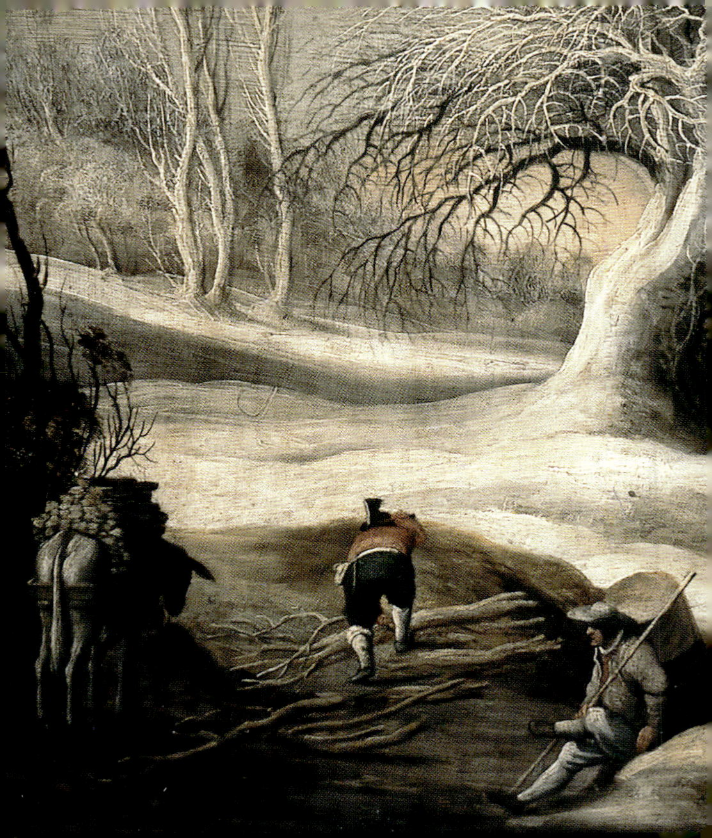

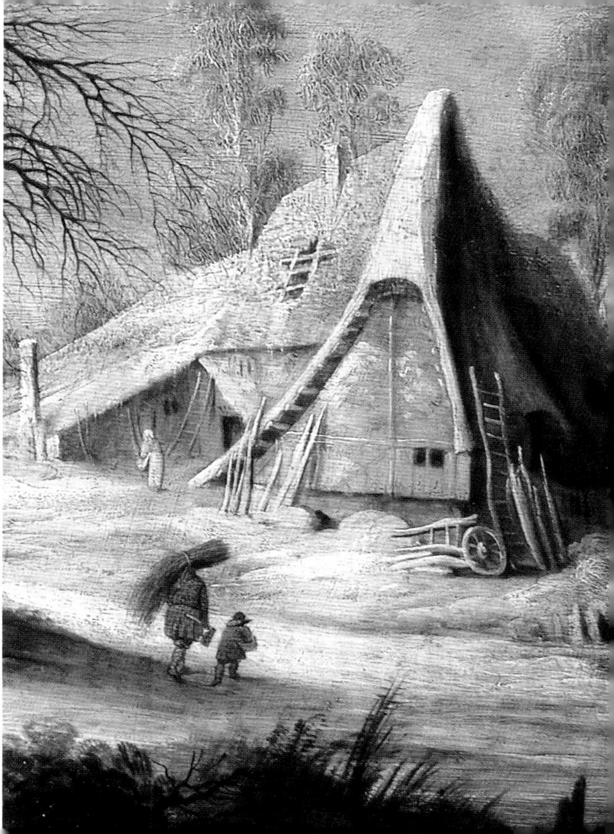

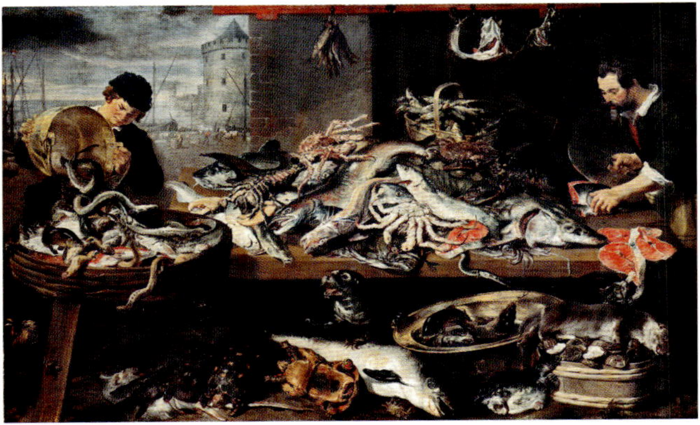

Frans Snyders
Fish Stall
Early 17th century. Flanders

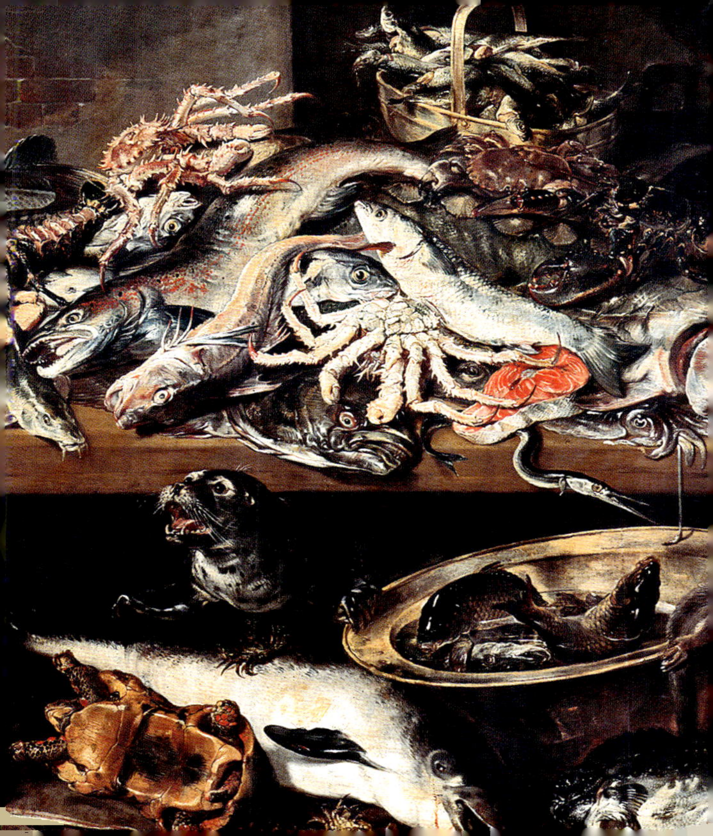

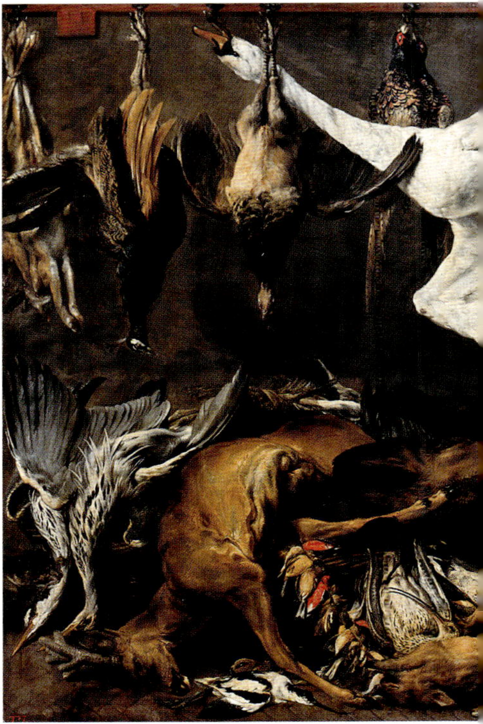

Frans Snyders
Game Stall
Early 17th century
Flanders

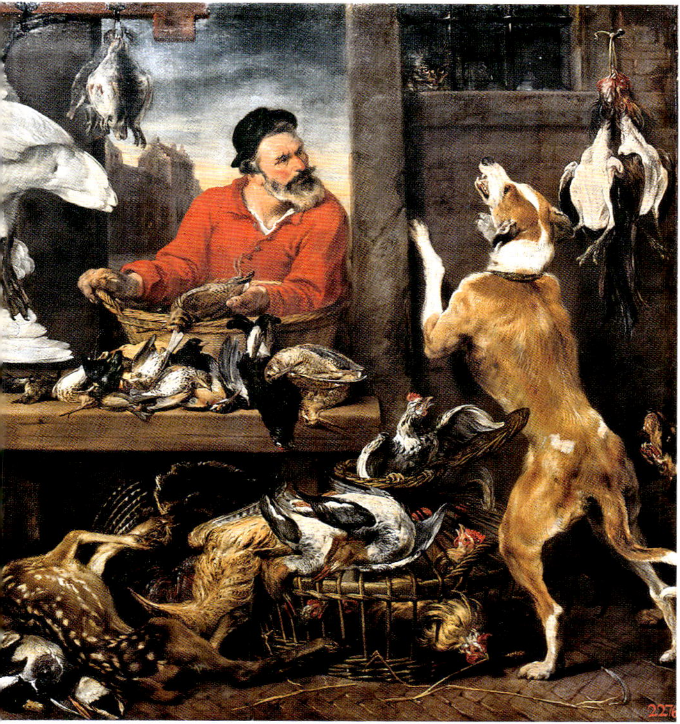

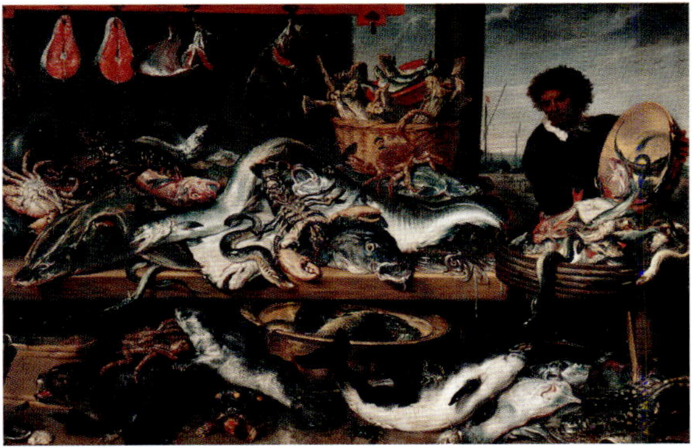

Frans Snyders
Fish Stall
Early 17th century. Flanders

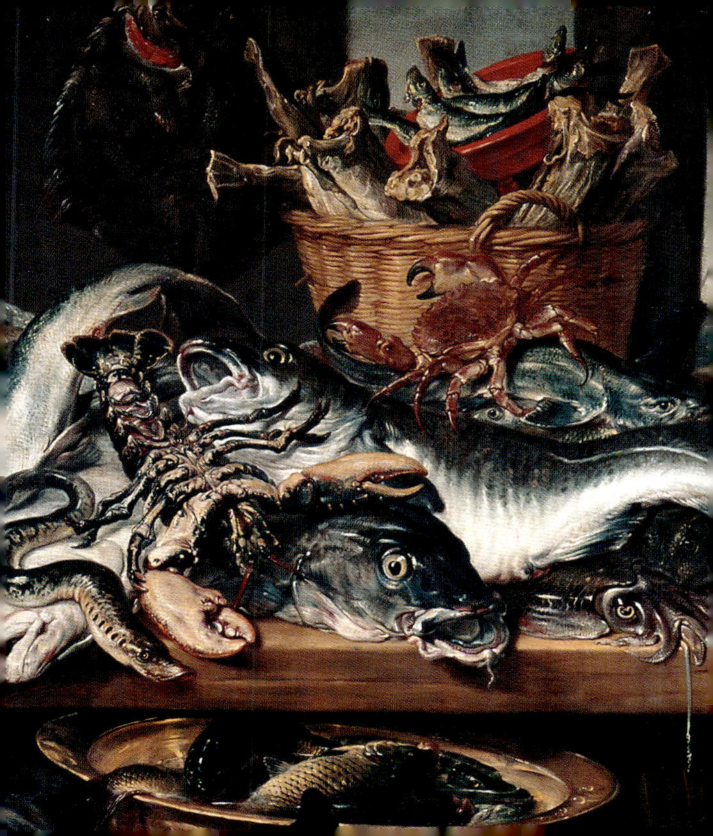

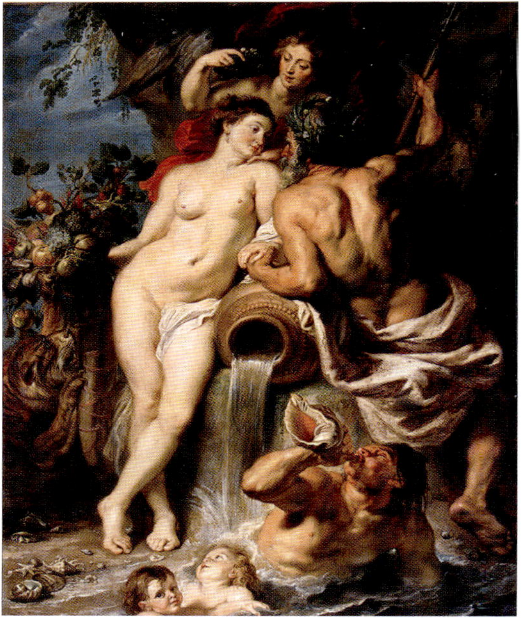

Pieter Paul Rubens
The Union of Earth and Water
Circa 1618. Flanders

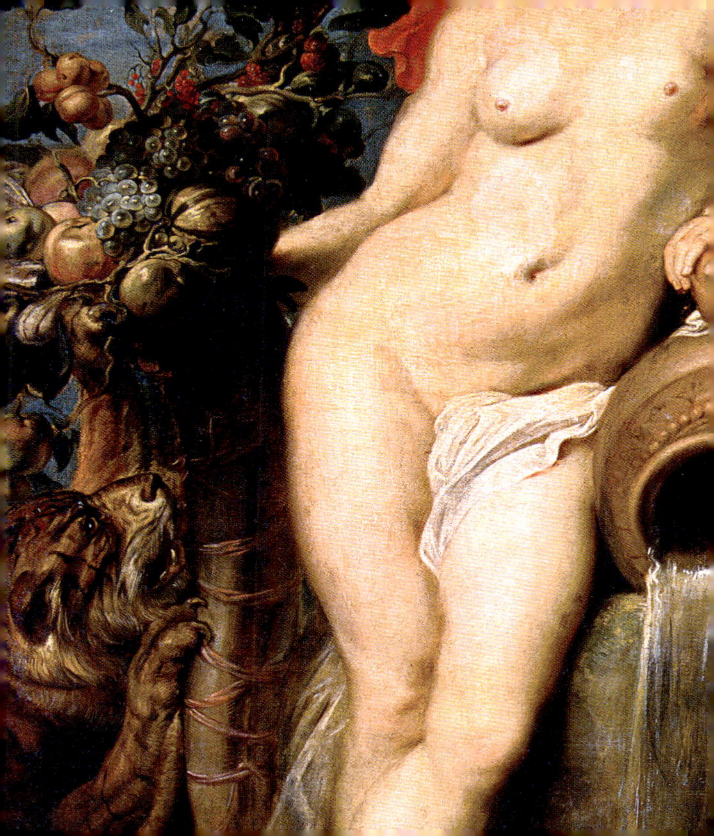

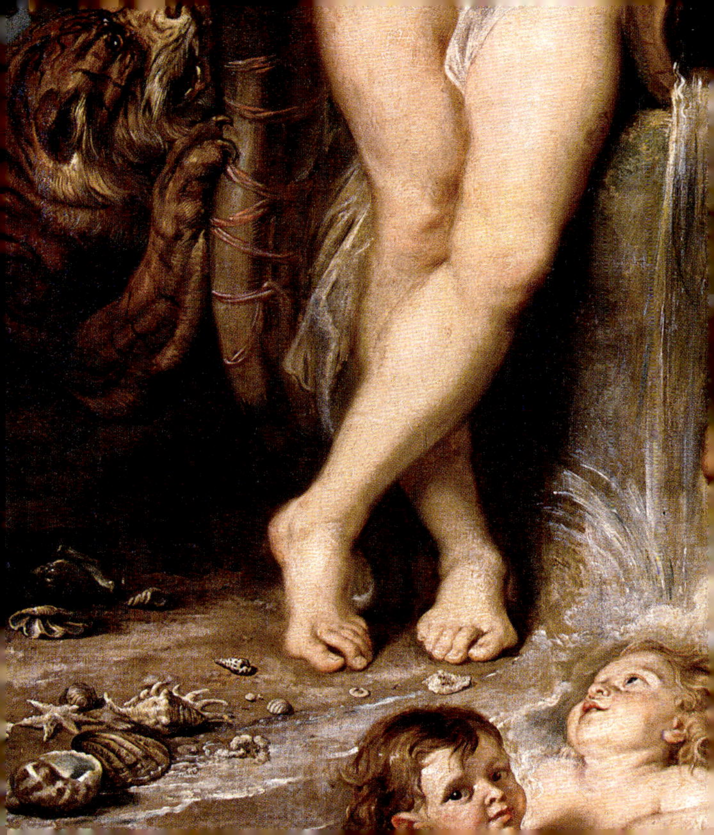

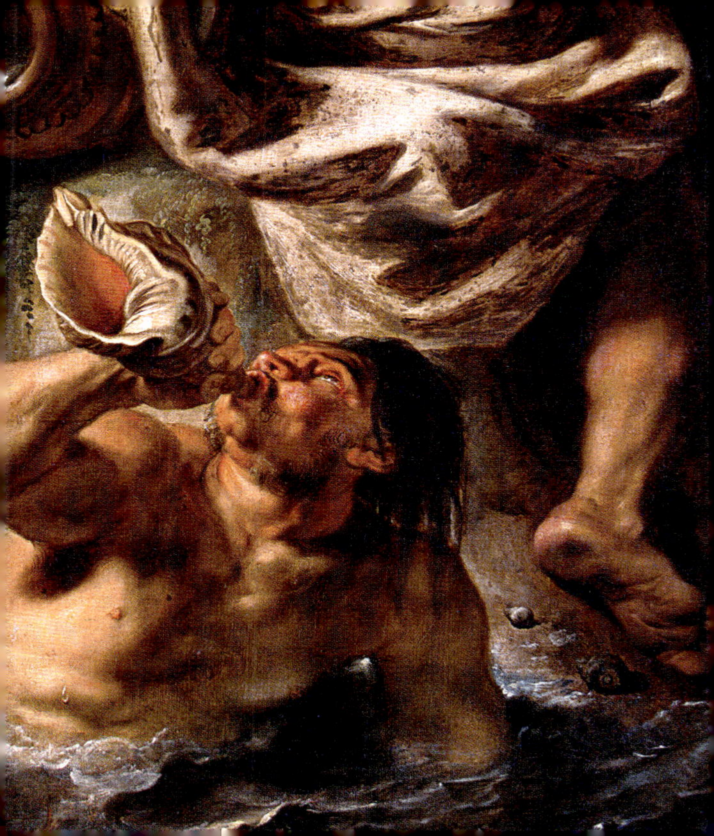

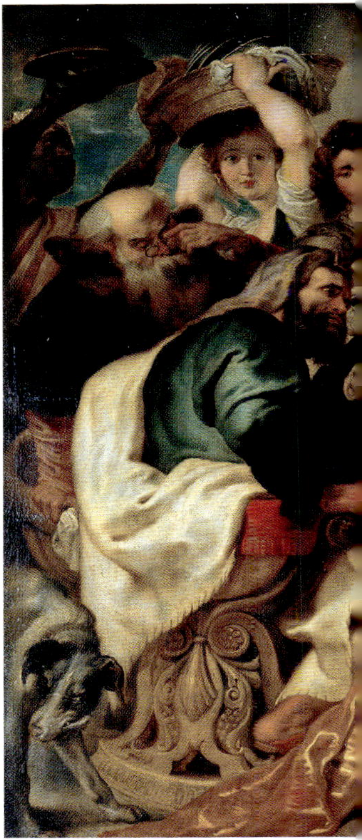

Pieter Paul Rubens
The Feast in the House of Simon the Pharisee
Between 1618 and 1620. Flanders

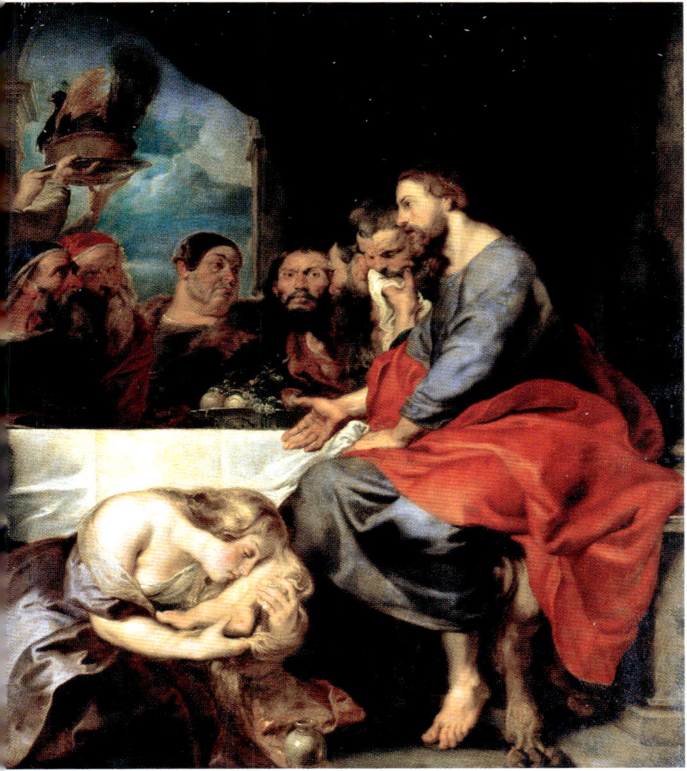

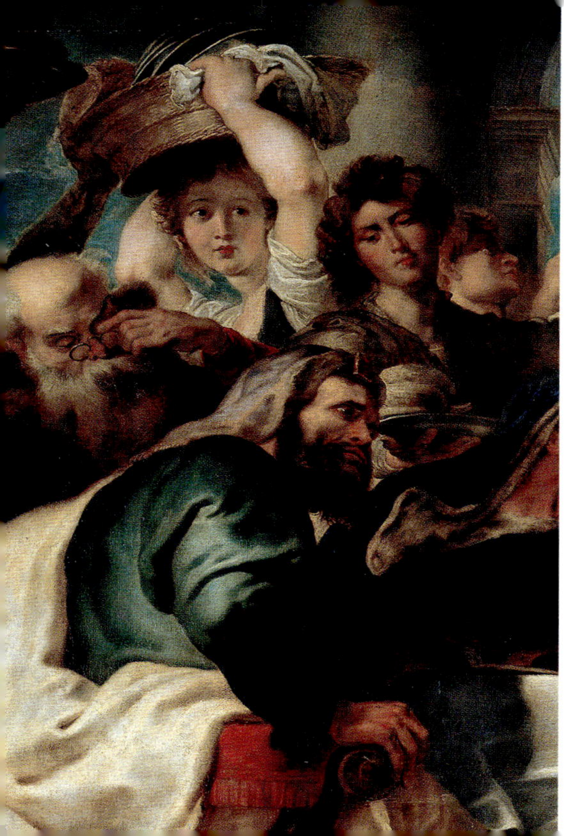

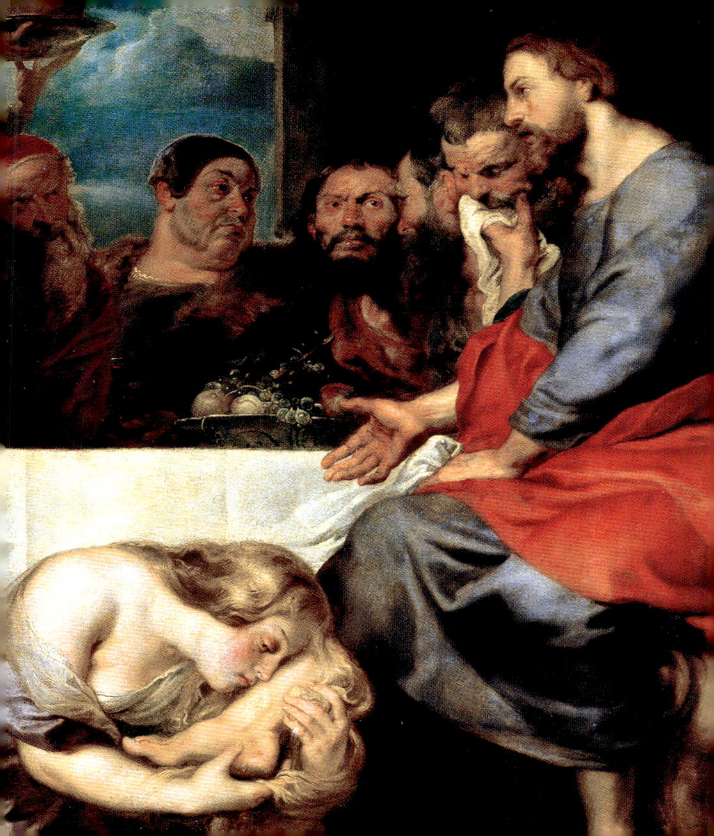

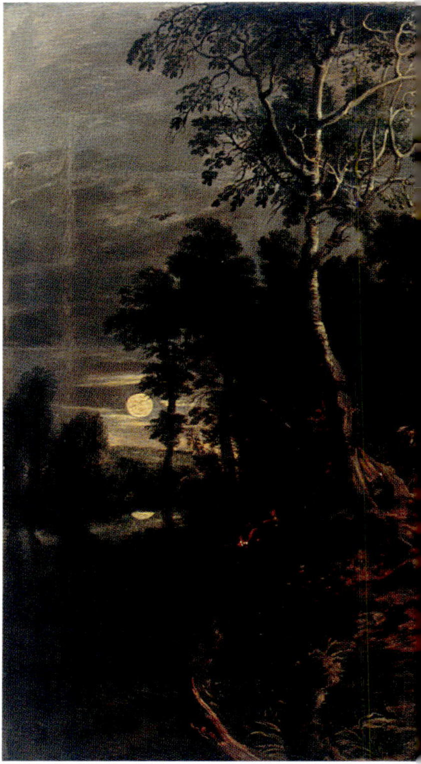

Pieter Paul Rubens
Landscape with Stone Carriers
Circa 1620. Flanders

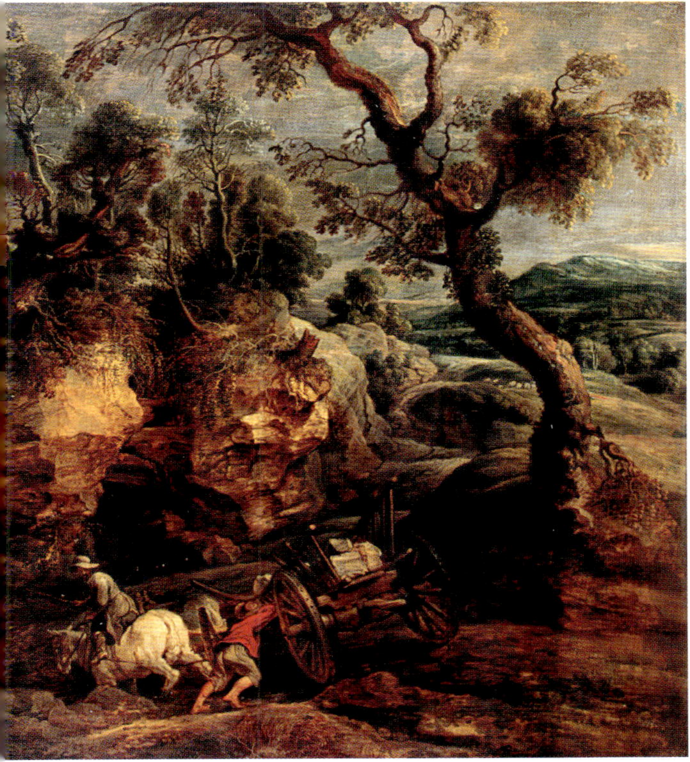

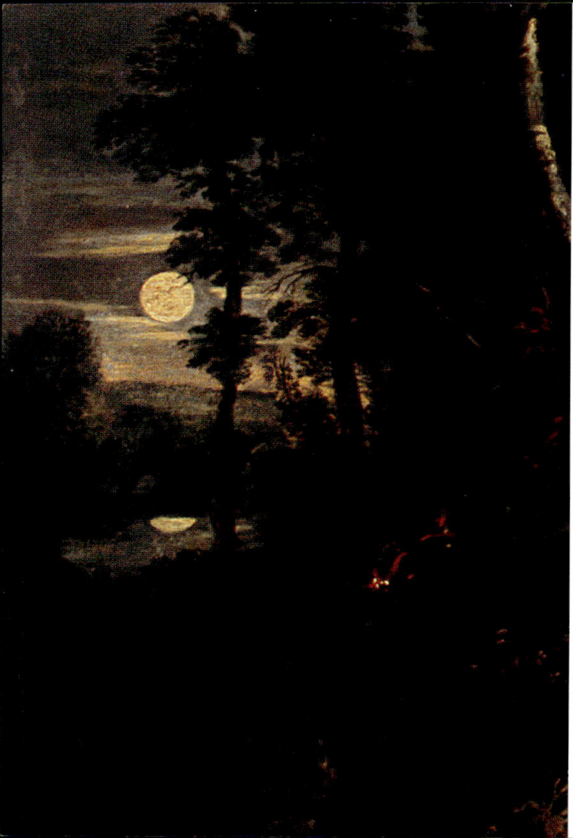

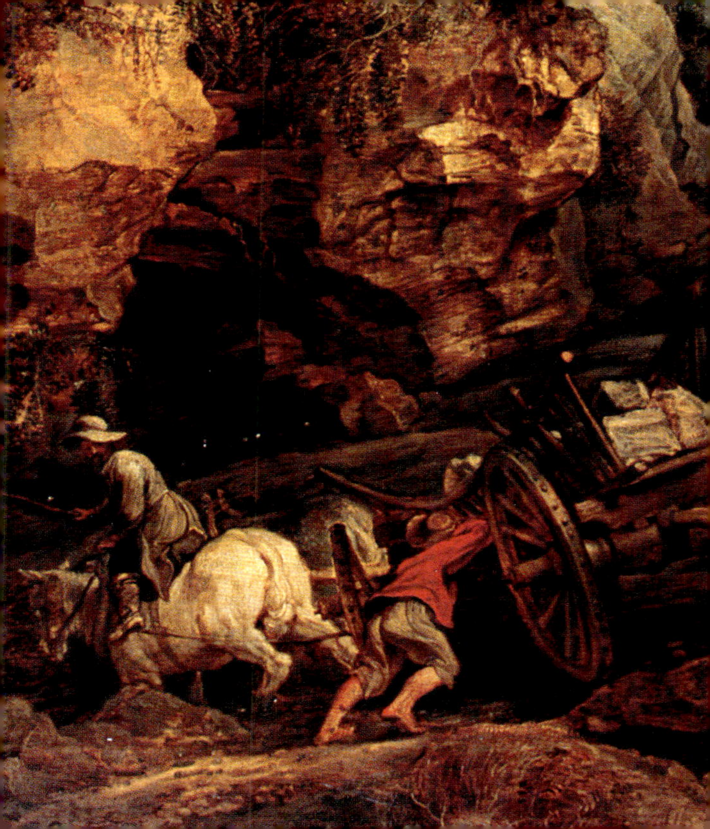

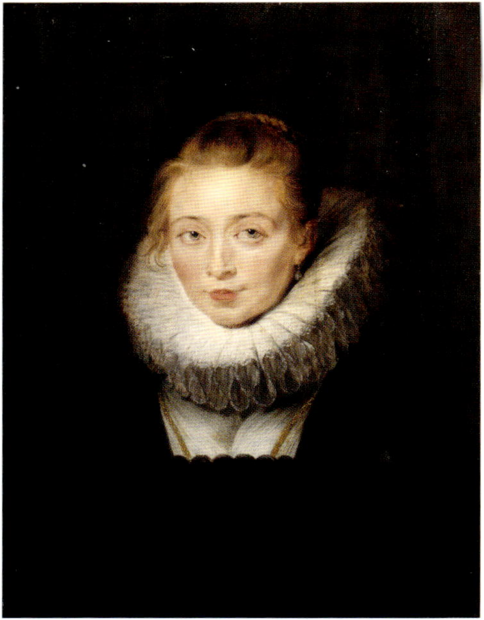

Pieter Paul Rubens
Portrait of Lady-in-Waiting to the Infanta Isabella
Middle 1620s. Flanders

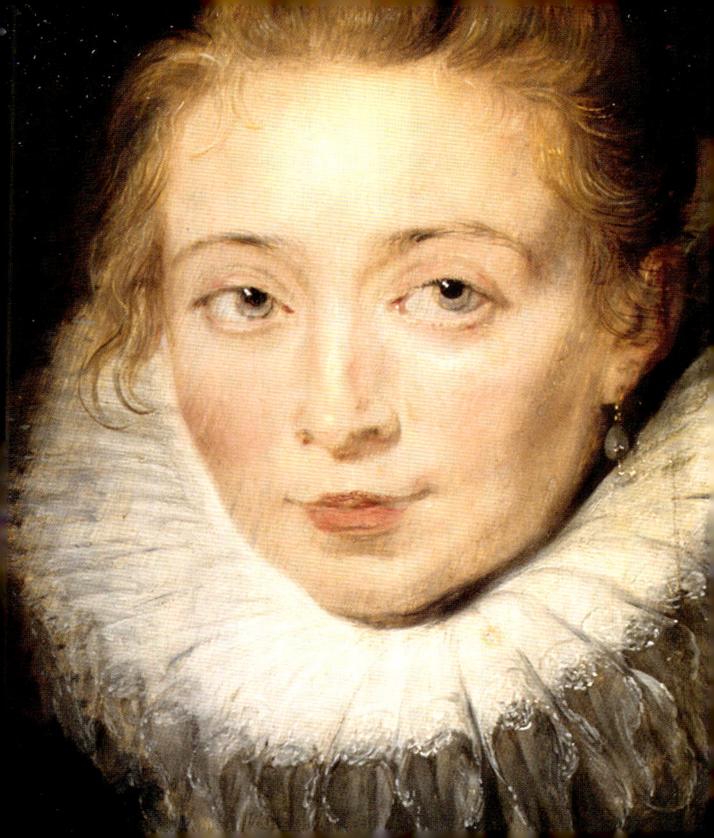

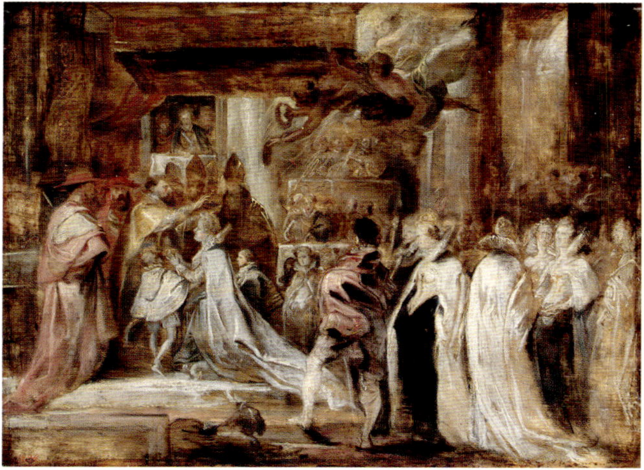

Pieter Paul Rubens
The Coronation of Maria de' Medici
1622. Flanders

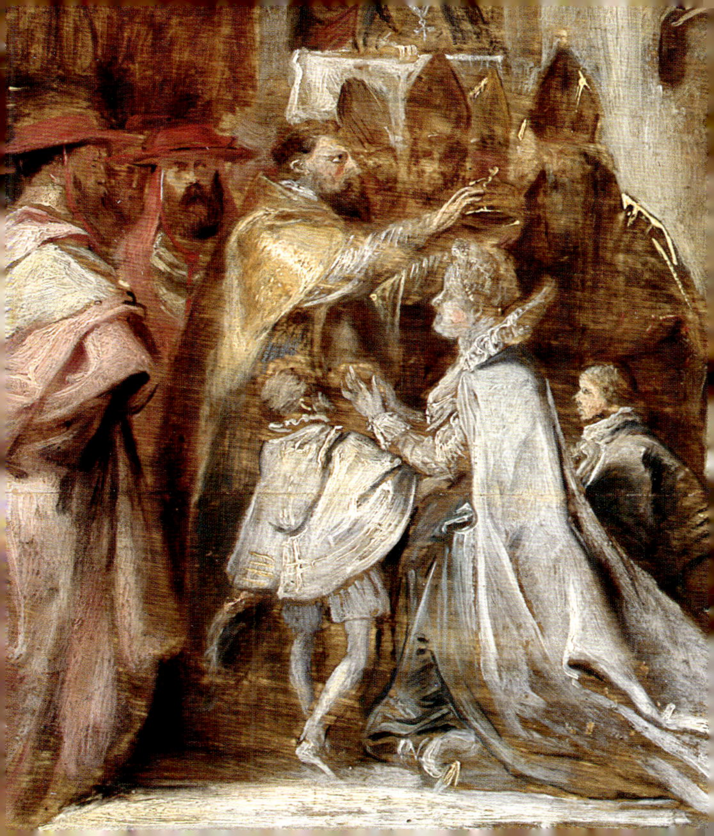

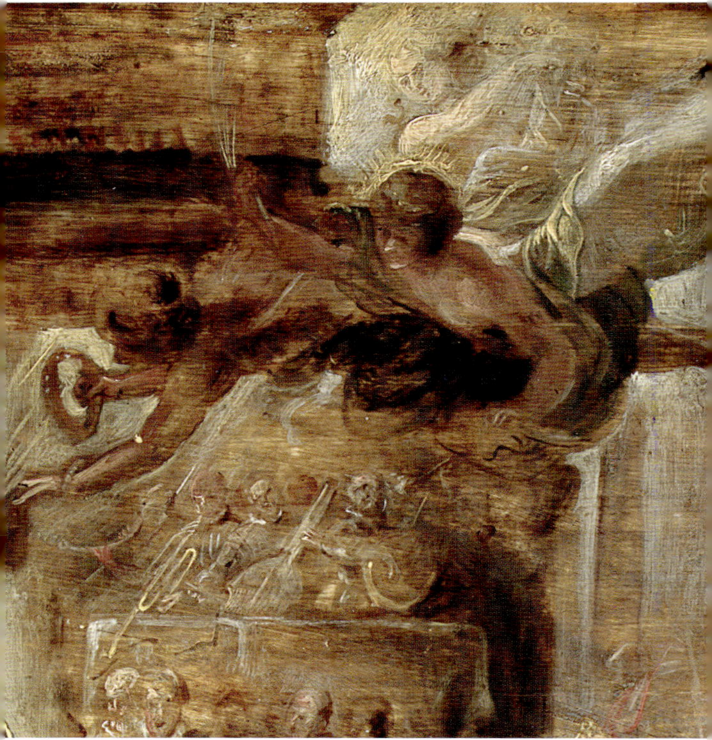

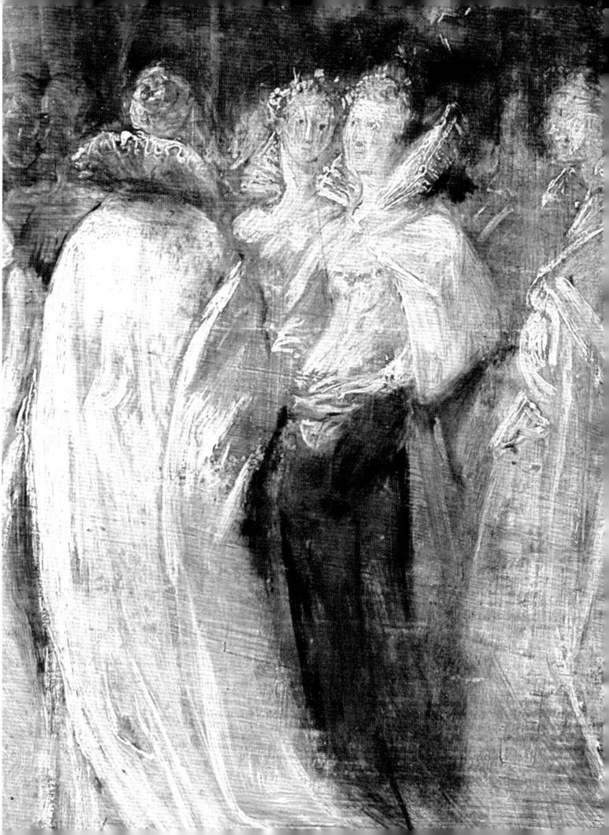

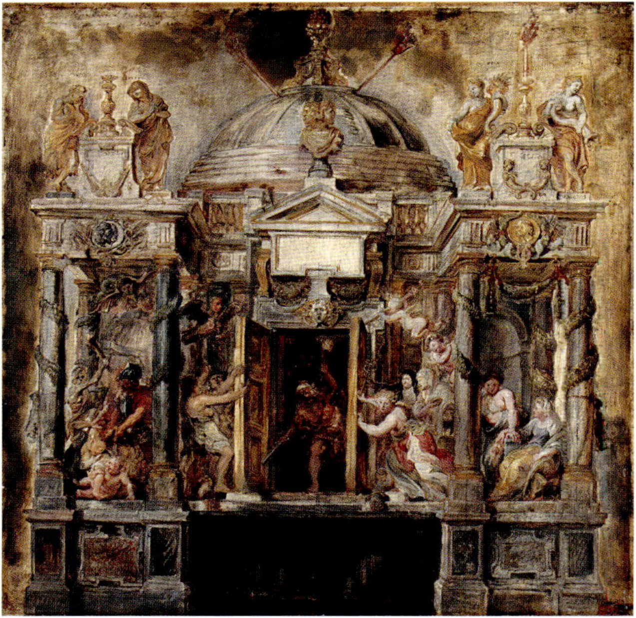

Pieter Paul Rubens
Temple of Janus
1634. Flanders

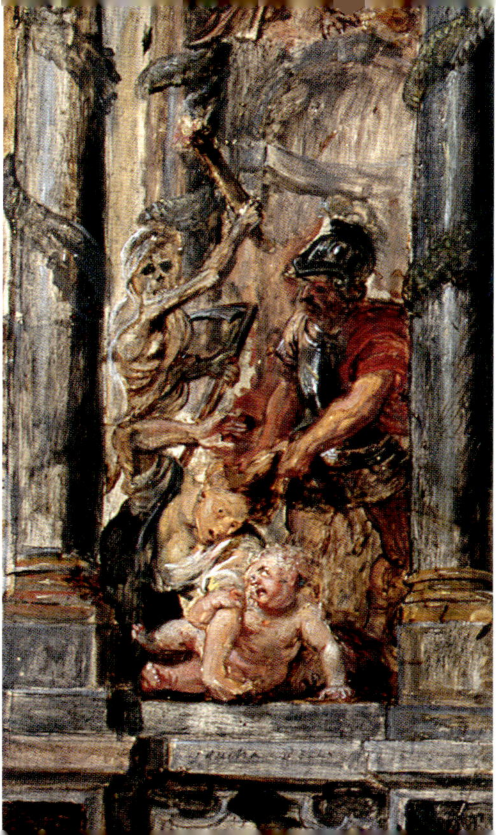

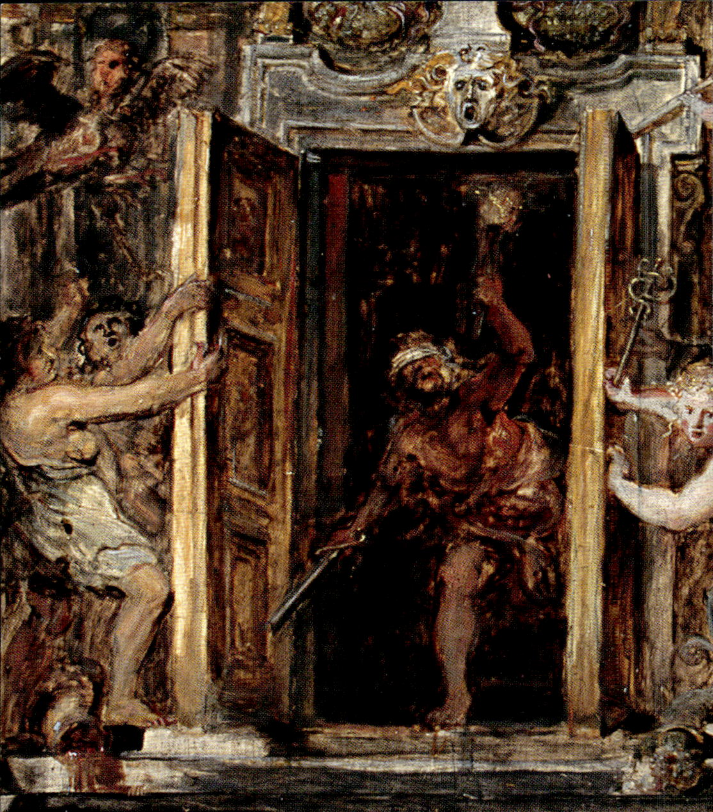

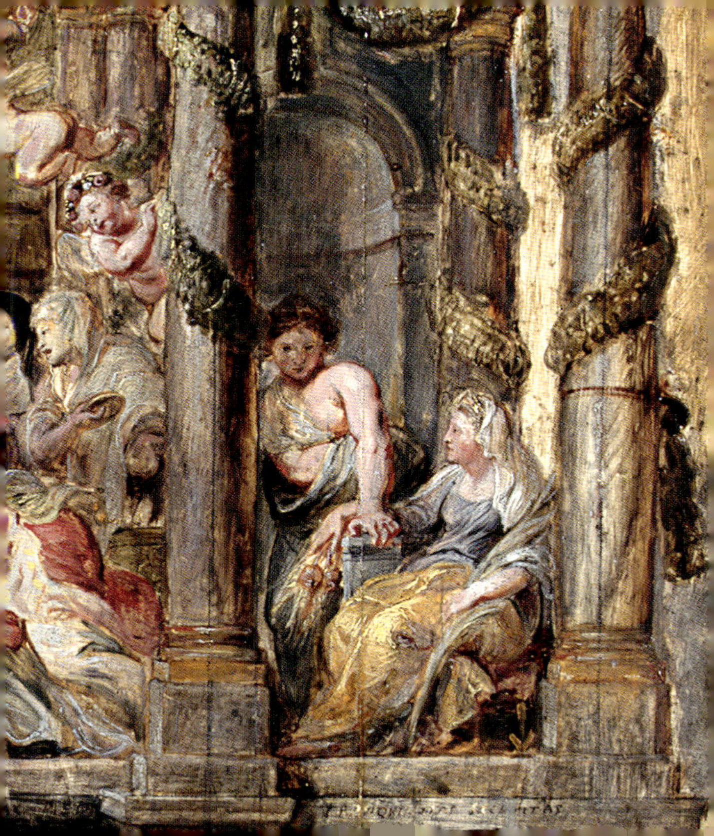

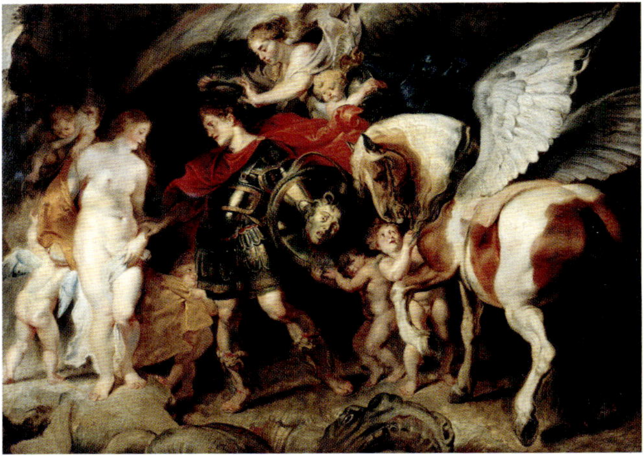

Pieter Paul Rubens
Perseus and Andromeda
Circa 1622. Flanders

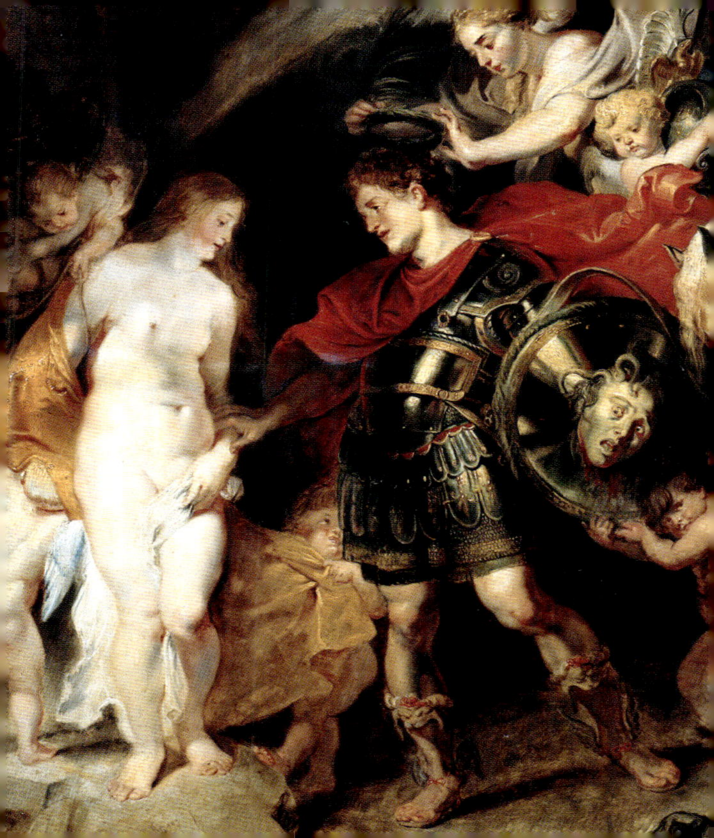

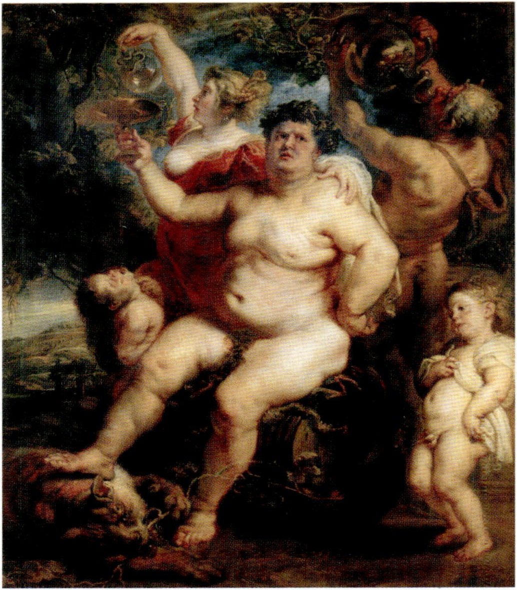

Pieter Paul Rubens
Bacchus
Between 1638 and 1640. Flanders

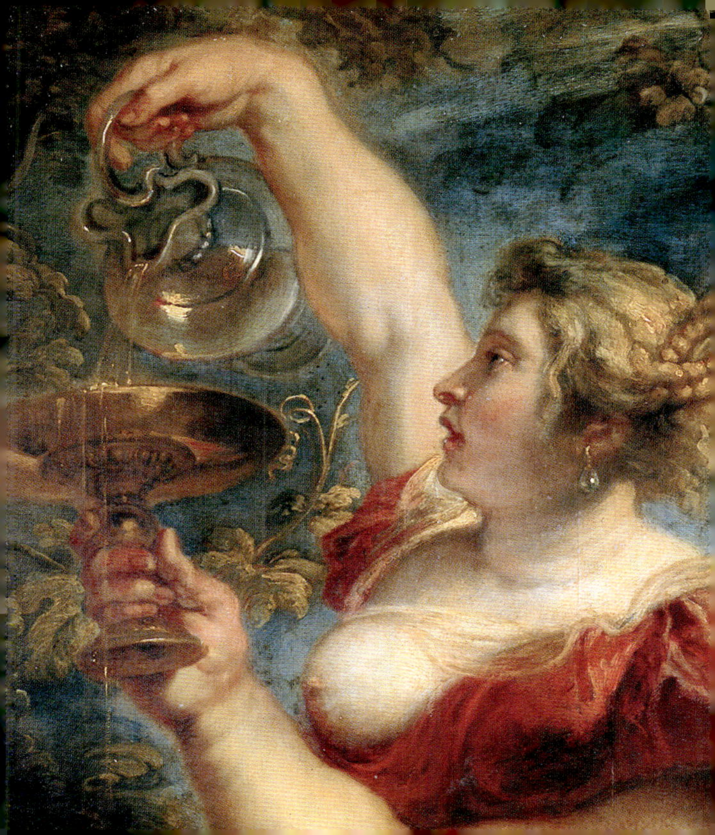

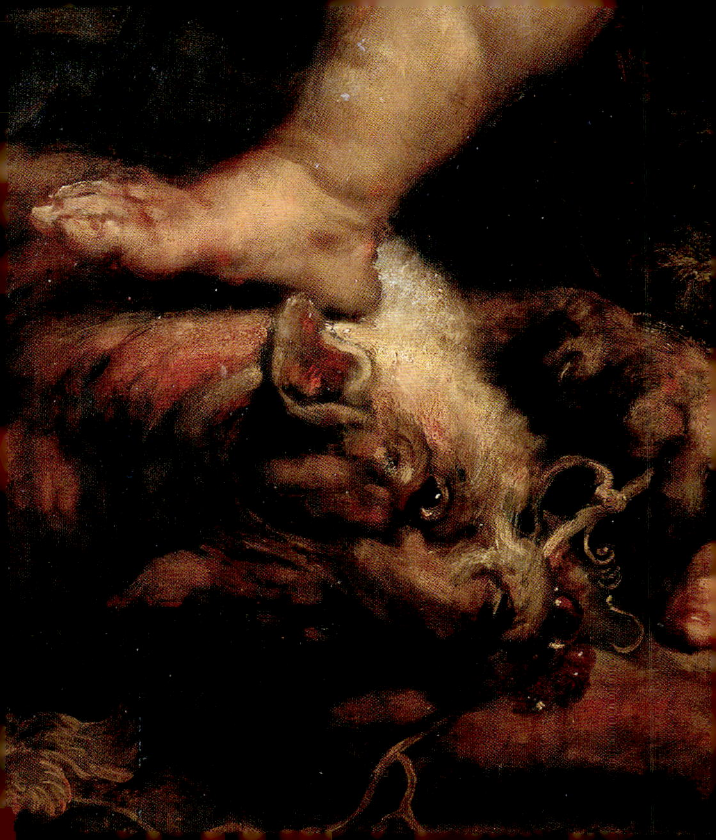

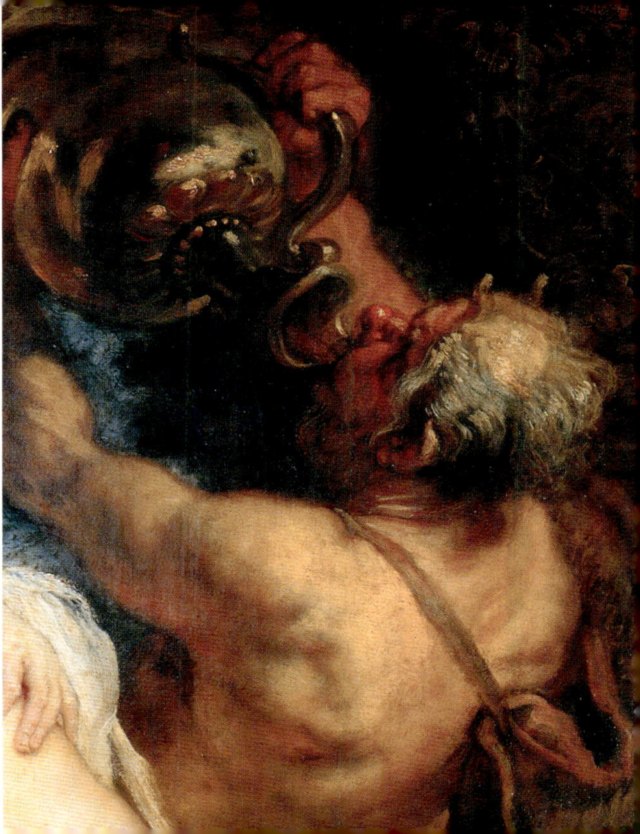

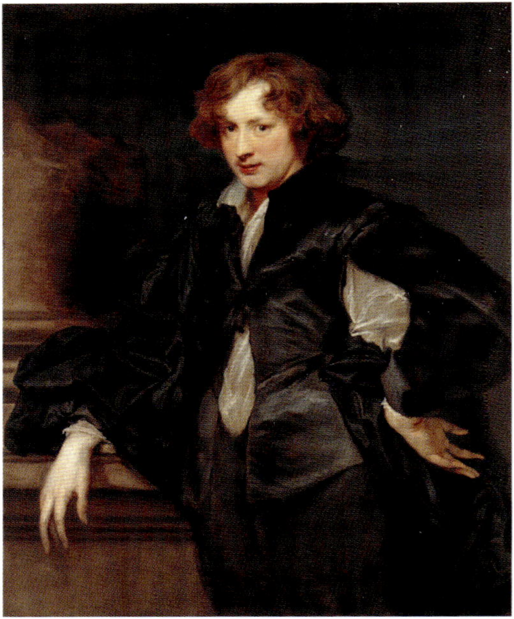

Anthony van Dyck
Self-Portrait
Late 1620s – early 1630s. Flanders

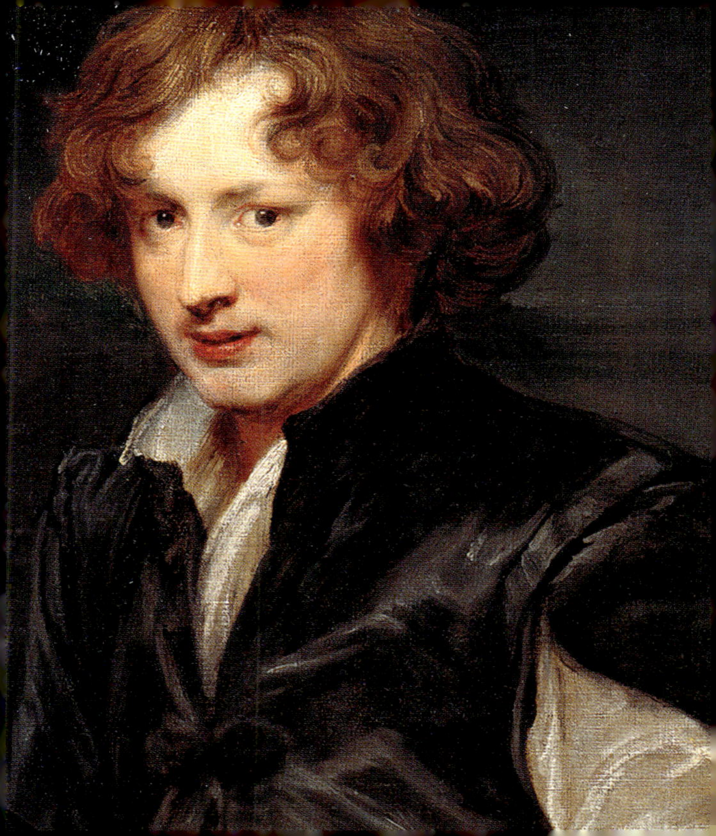

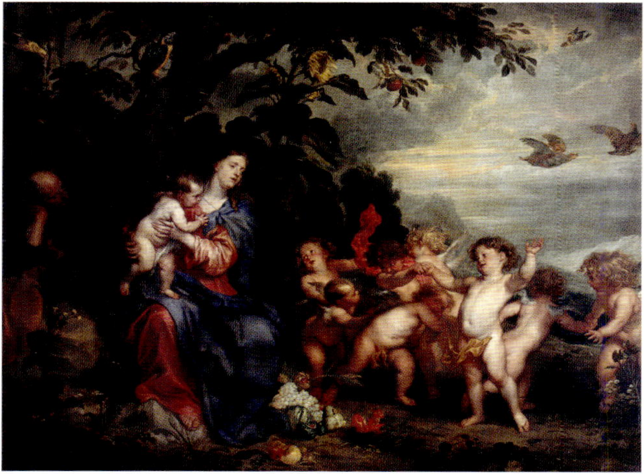

Anthony van Dyck
Madonna with Partridges
Circa 1630–32. Flanders

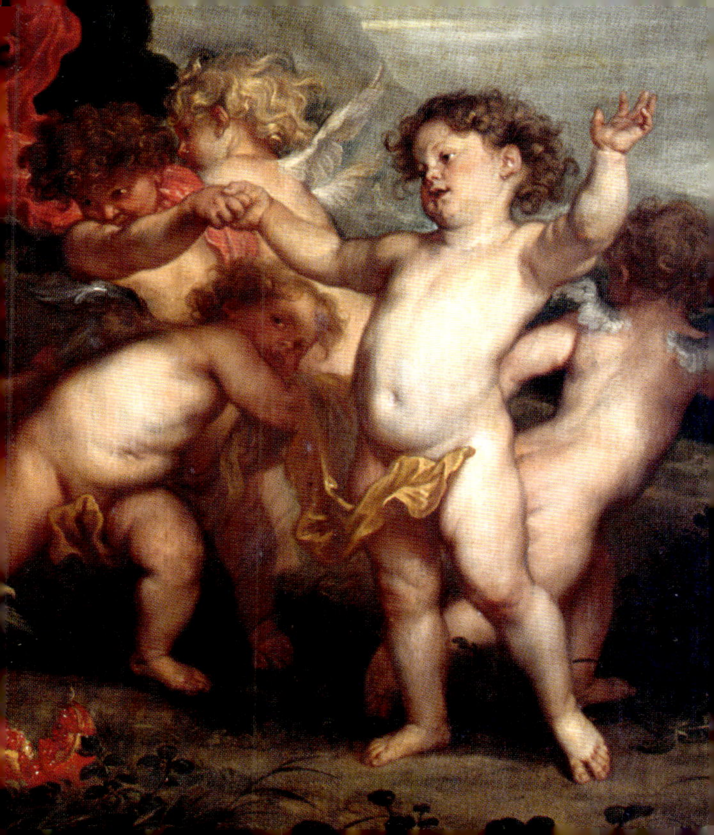

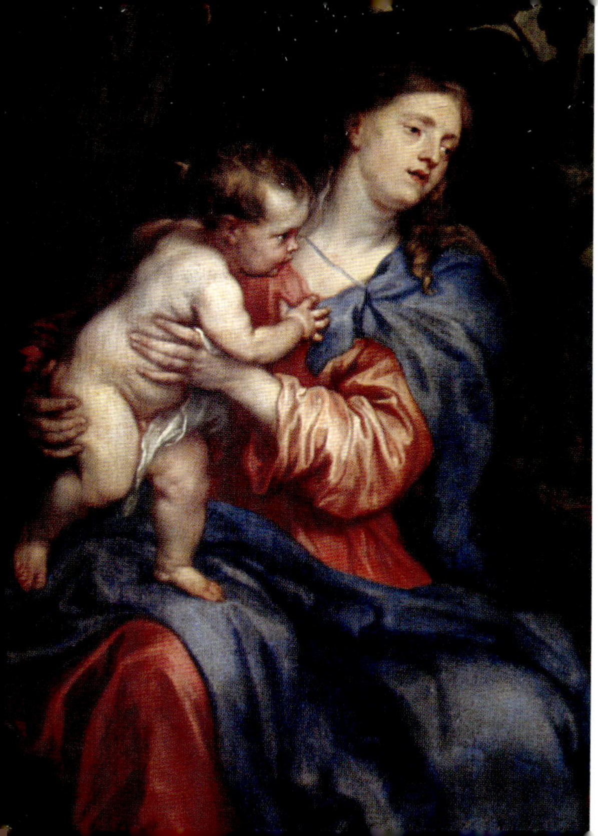

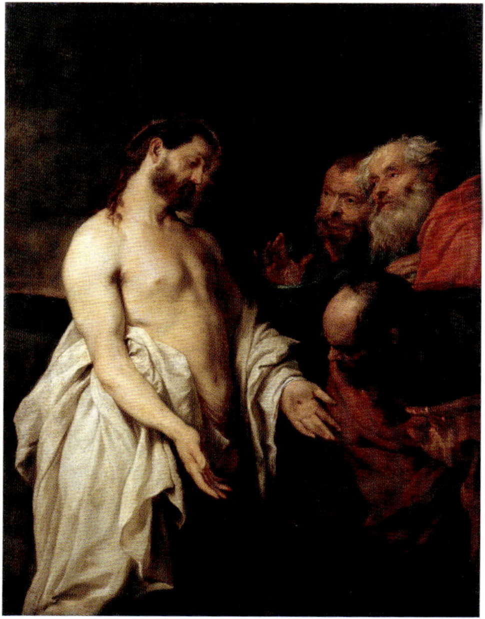

Anthony van Dyck
The Appearance of Christ to His Disciples
1625–26. Flanders

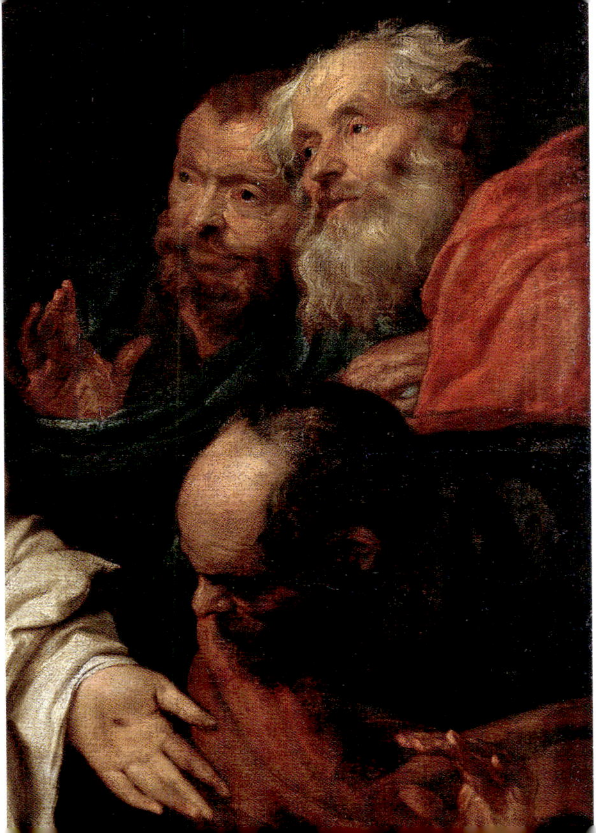

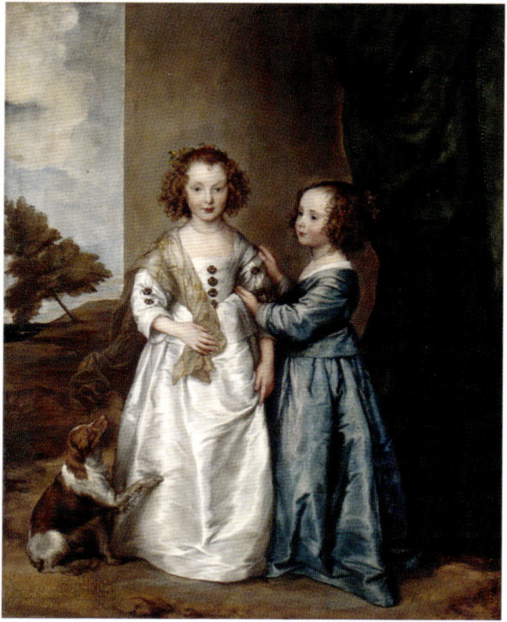

Anthony van Dyck
Portrait of Philadelphia and Elizabeth Wharton (?)
Late 1630s. Flanders

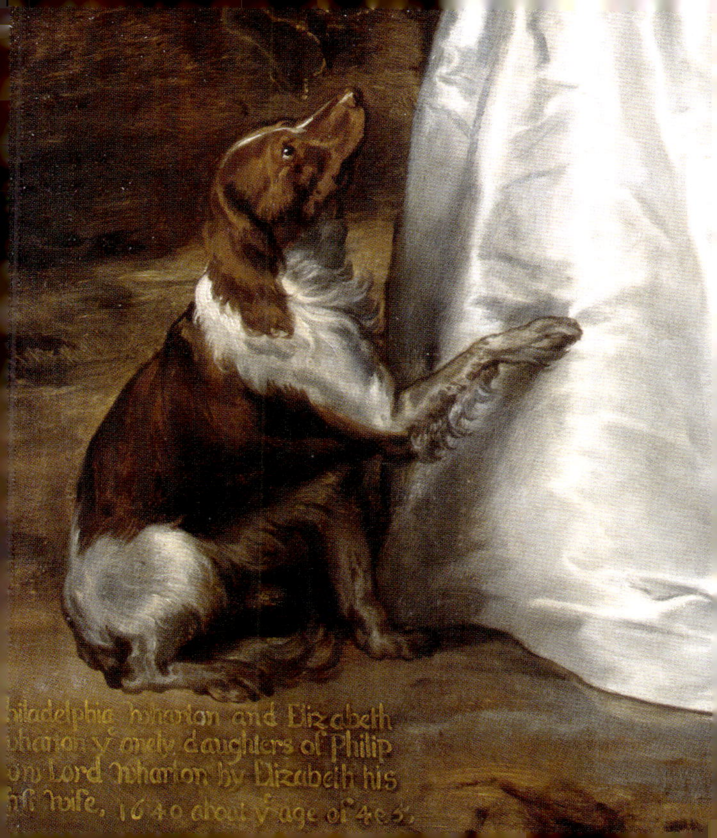
hiladelphia Wharton and Elizabeth
Wharton y onely daughters of Philip
Lord Wharton by Elizabeth his
wife, 1640 about y age of 4 & 5

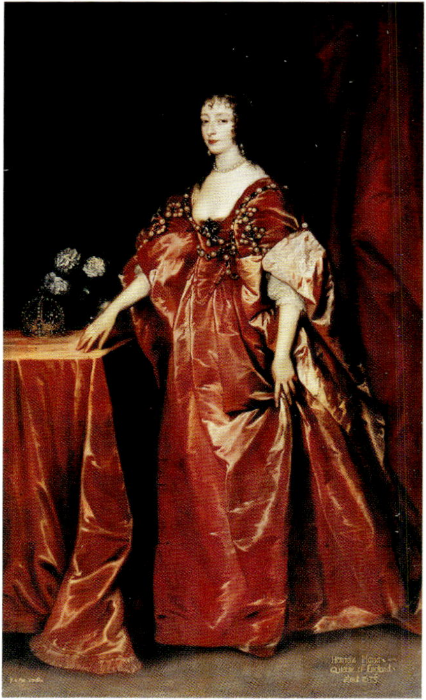

Anthony van Dyck
Portrait of Queen Henrietta-Maria
Circa 1638. Flanders

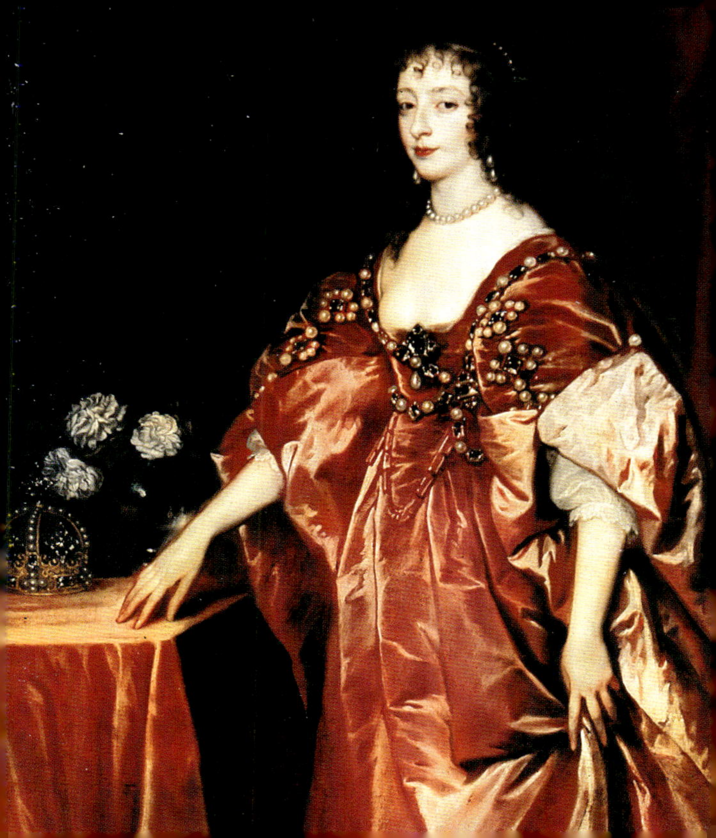

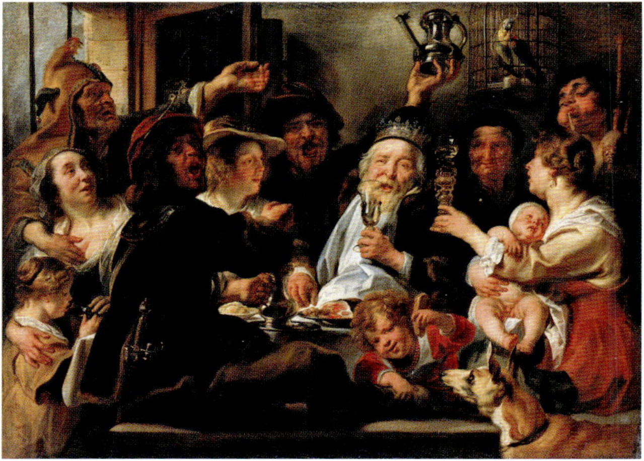

Jacob Jordaens
The Bean King
Circa 1638. Flanders

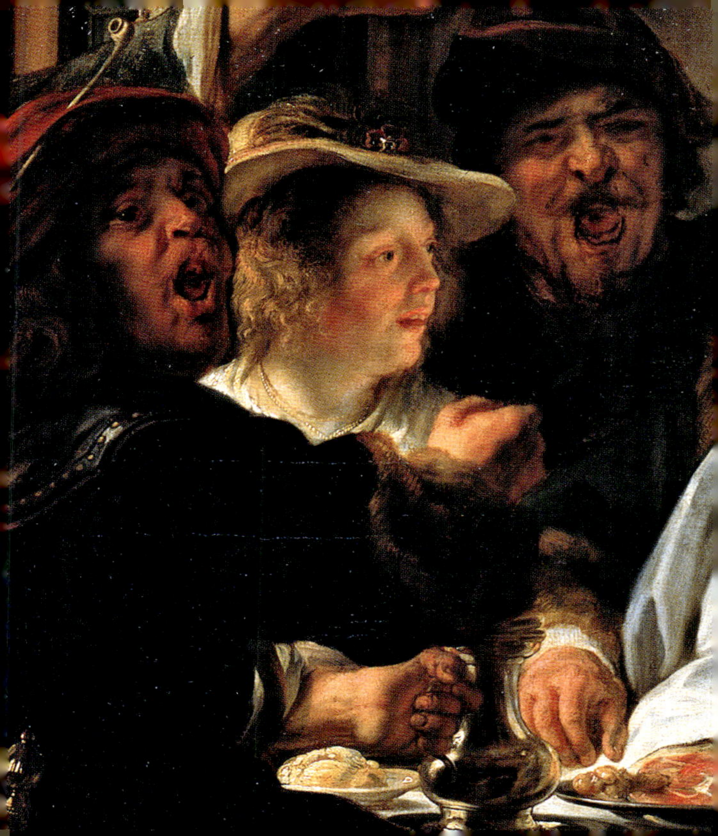

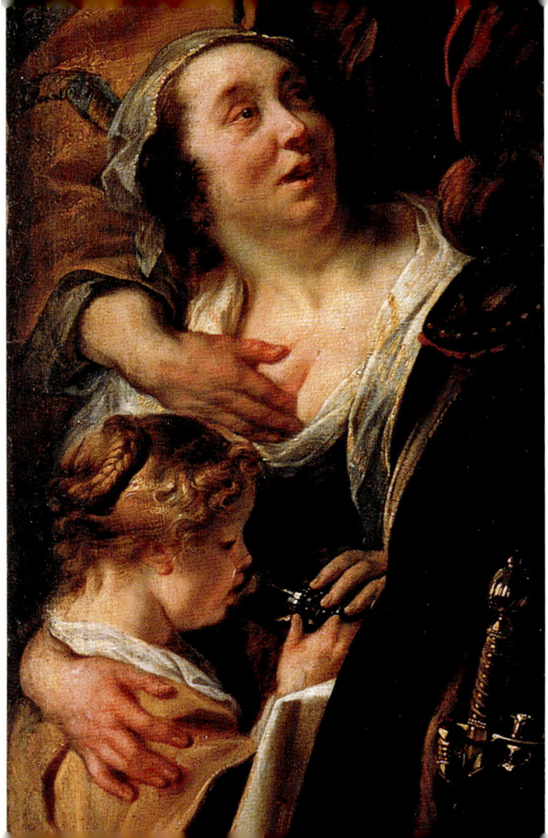

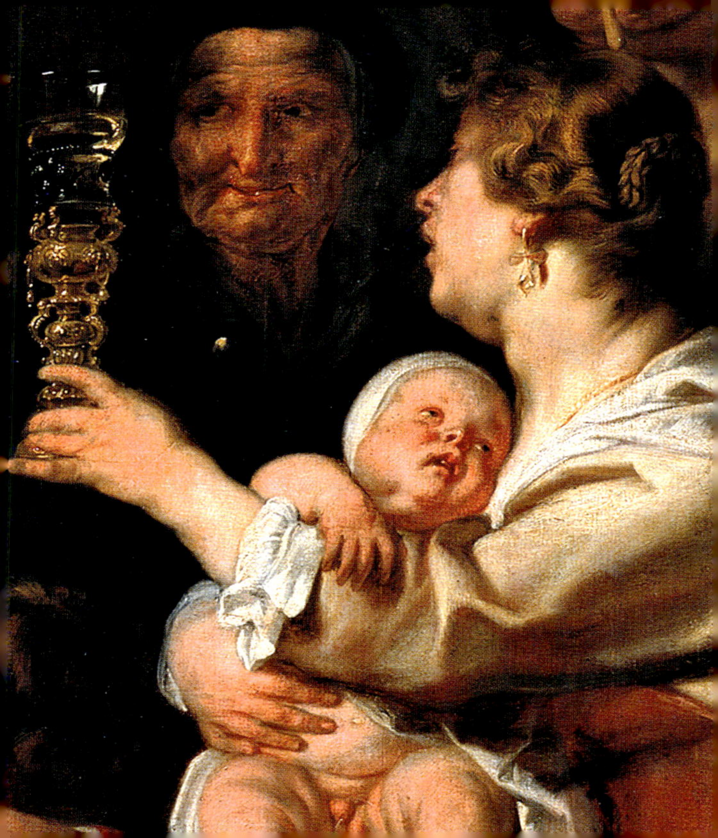

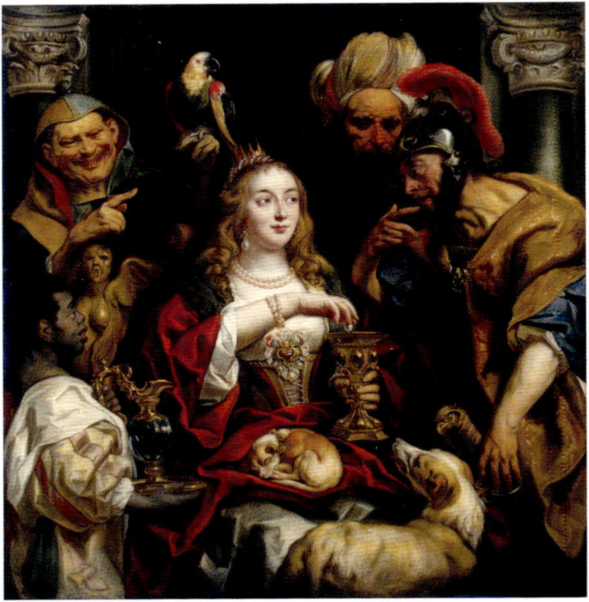

Jacob Jordaens
Cleopatra's Feast
1653. Flanders

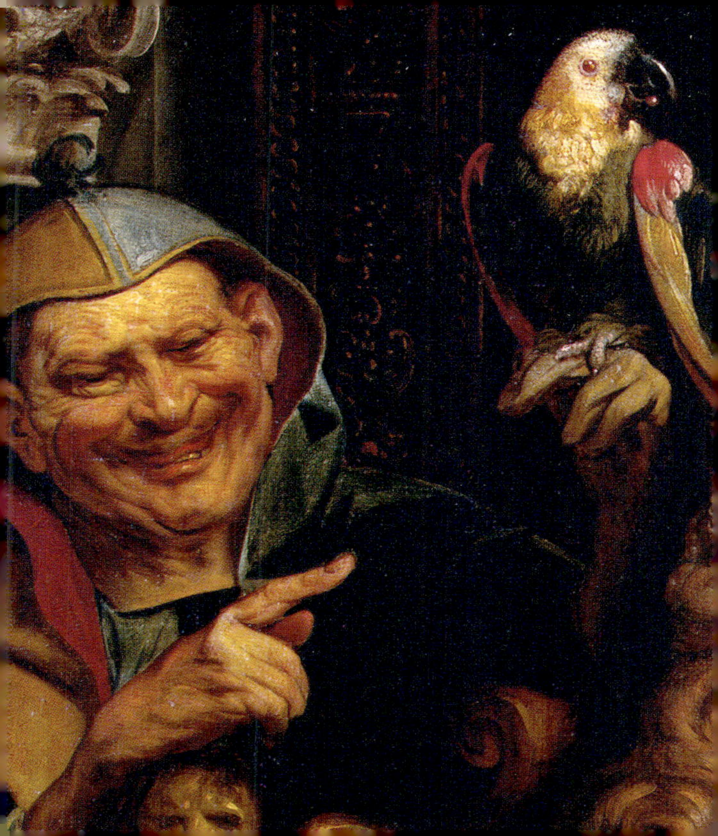

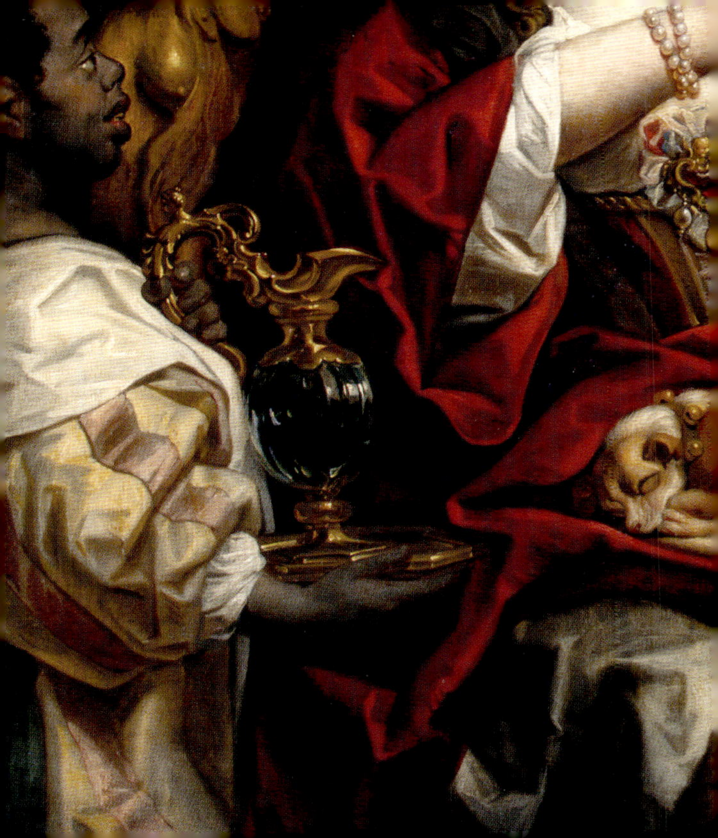

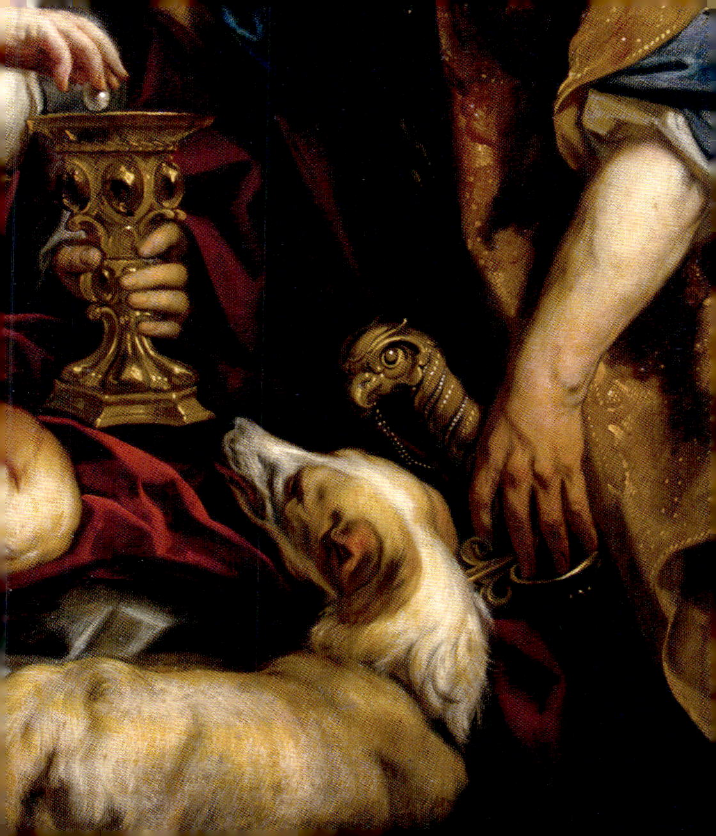

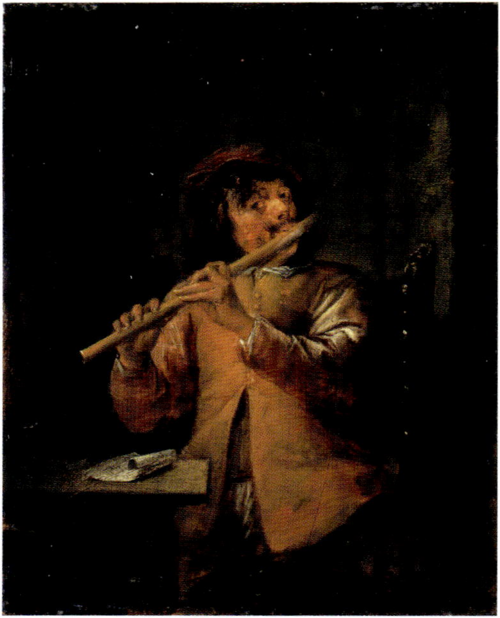

David Teniers the Younger
The Flute Player
Middle 1630s. Flanders

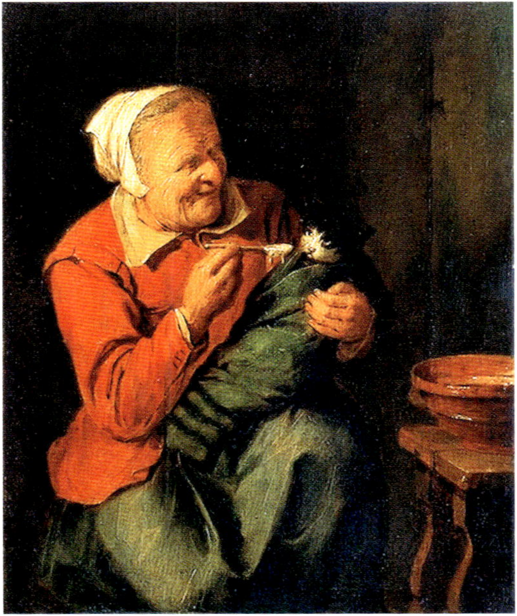

David Ryckaert III
Peasant Woman with a Cat
1640s. Flanders

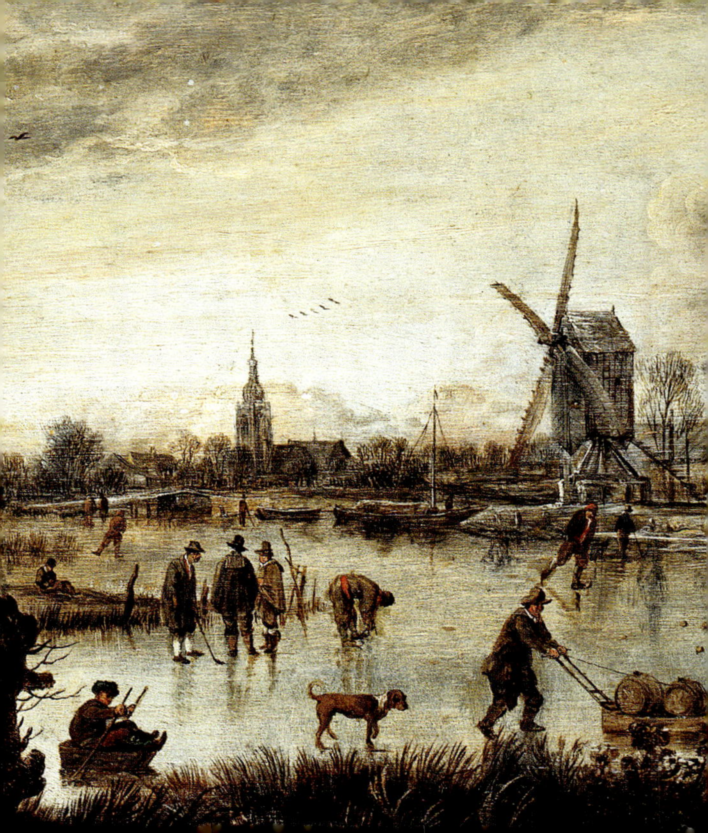

holland

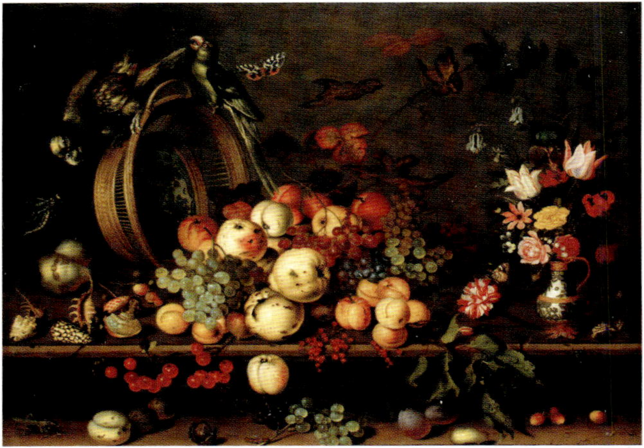

Balthasar van der Ast
Still Life with Fruits, Shells and Insects
1620s. Holland

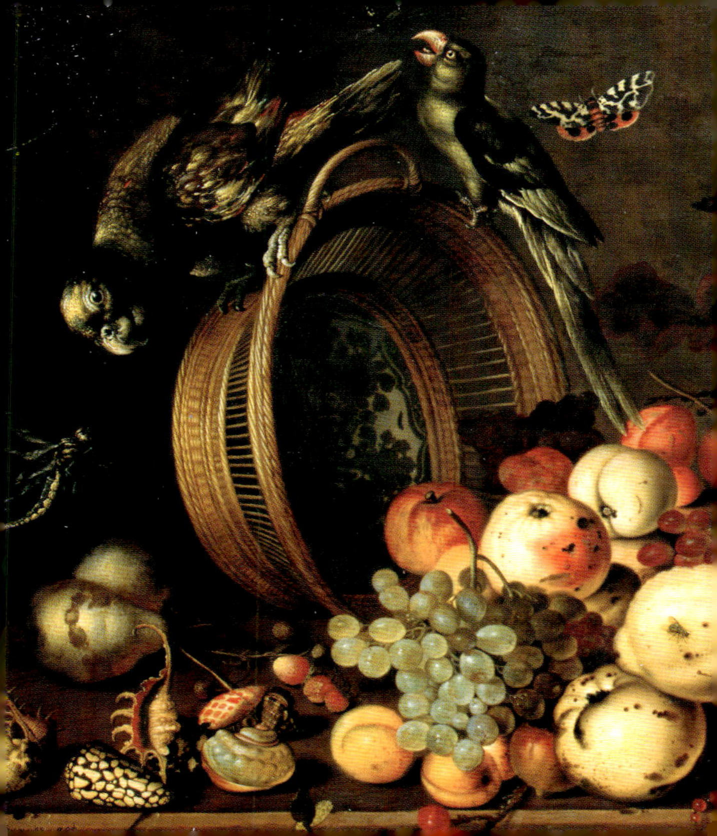

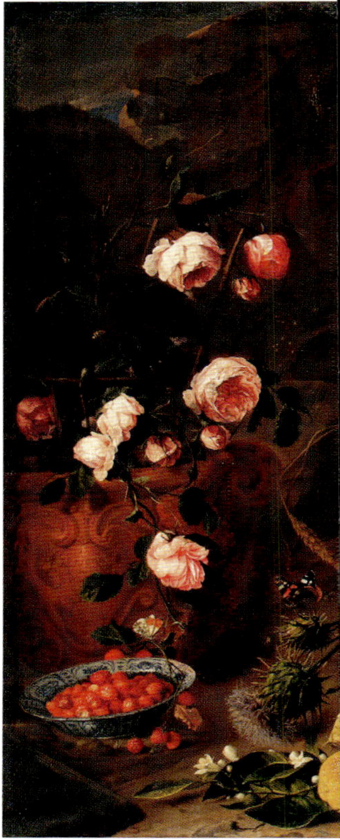

Jan Davidsz de Heem
Fruit and a Vase of Flowers
1655. Holland

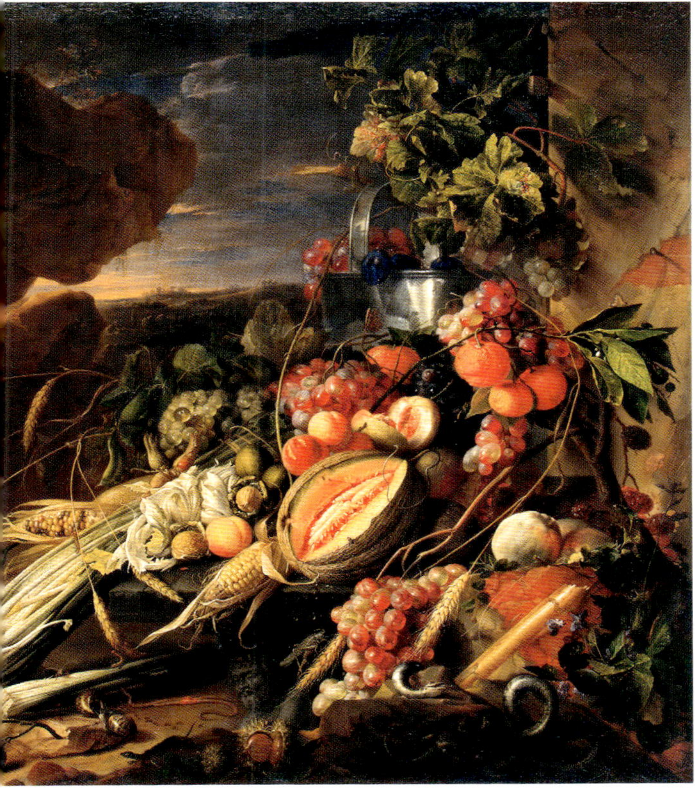

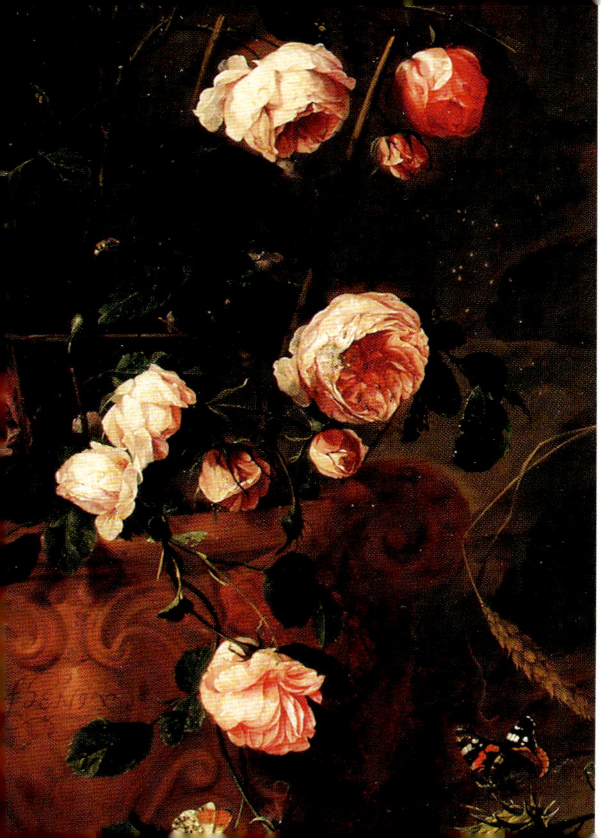

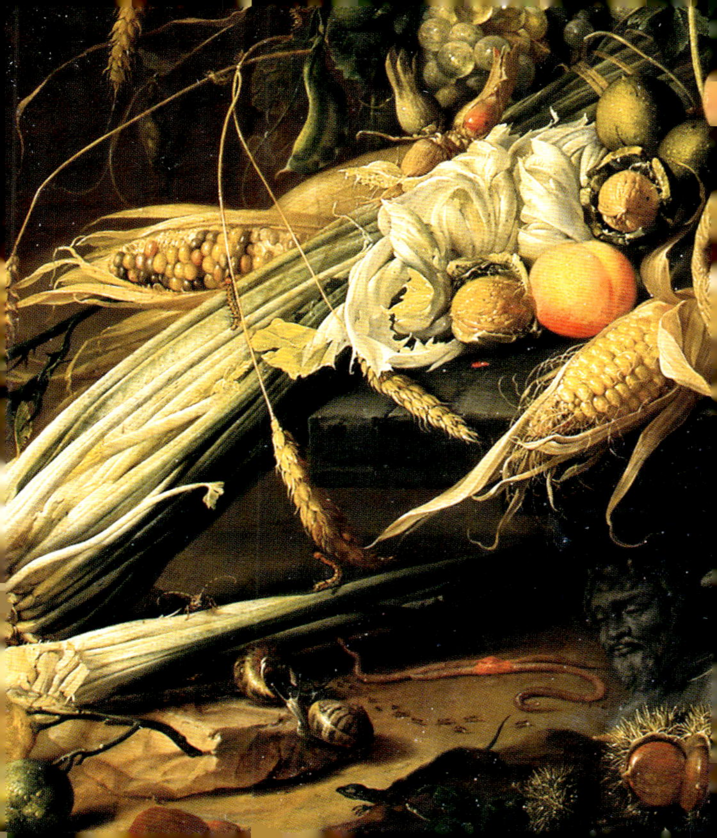

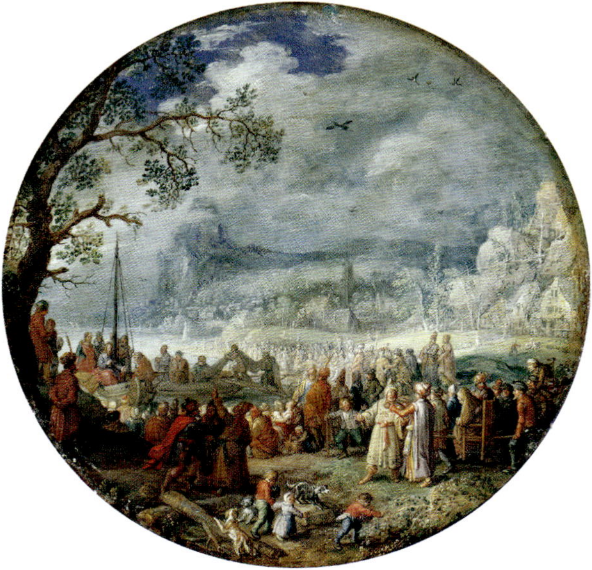

David Vinckeboons
The Sermon of Christ at Genezareth Lake
1623. Holland

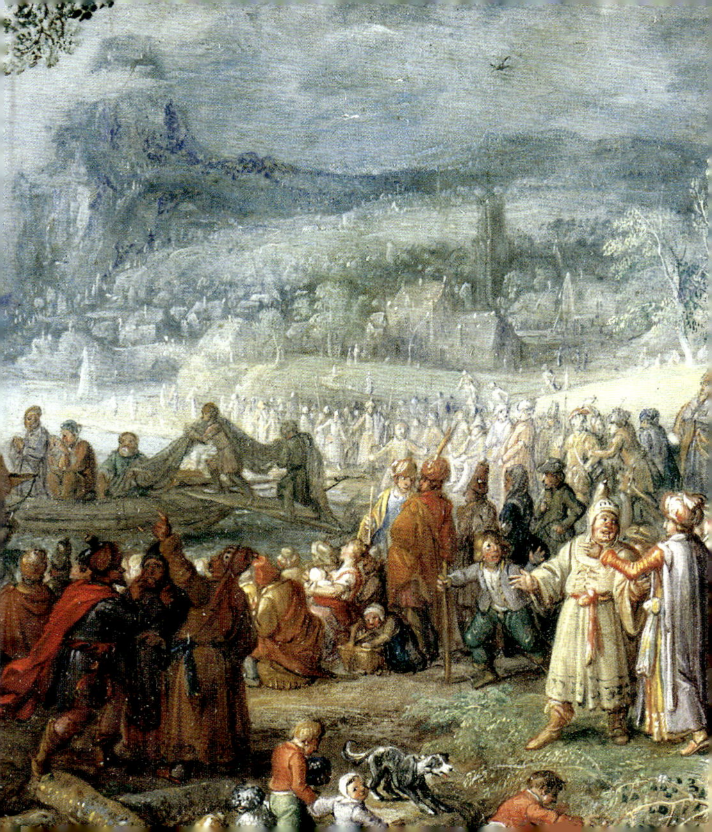

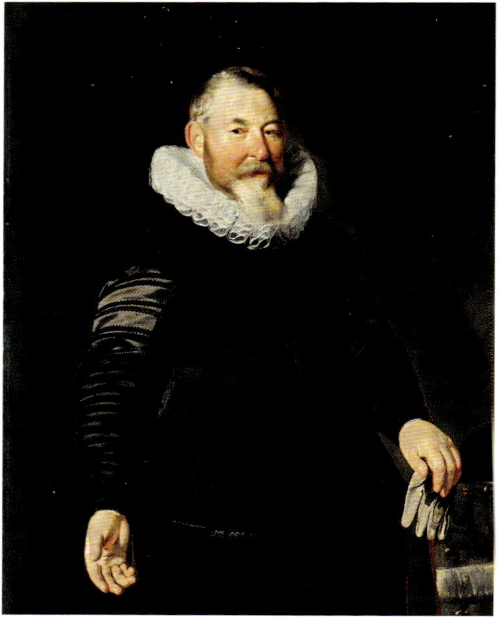

Thomas Hendricksz de Keyser
Portrait of a Man
1632. Holland

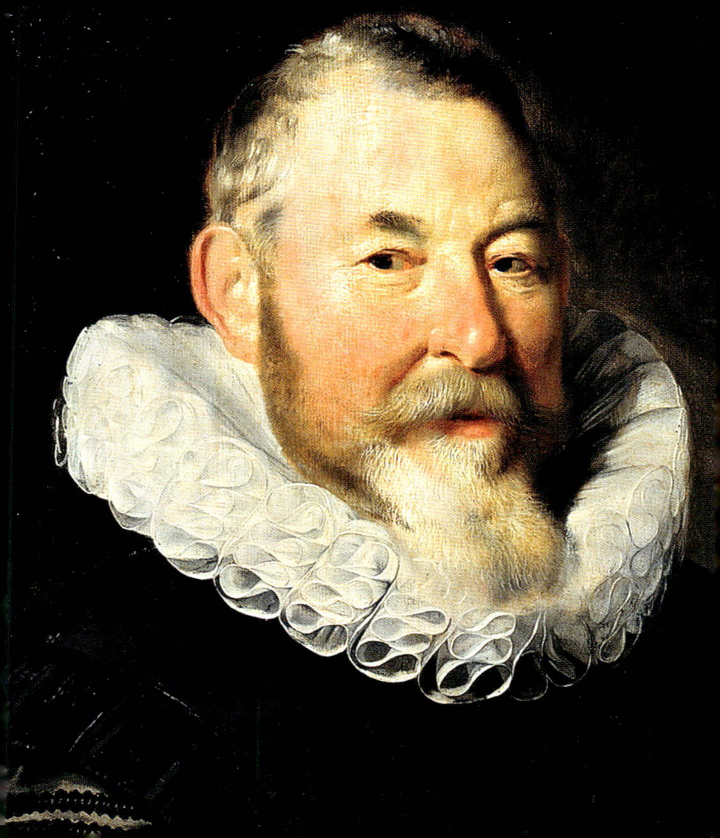

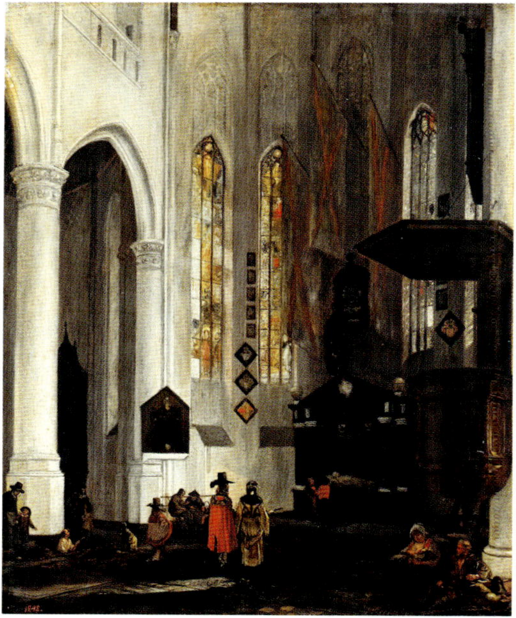

Emanuel de Witte
The Old Church in Delft
1626. Holland

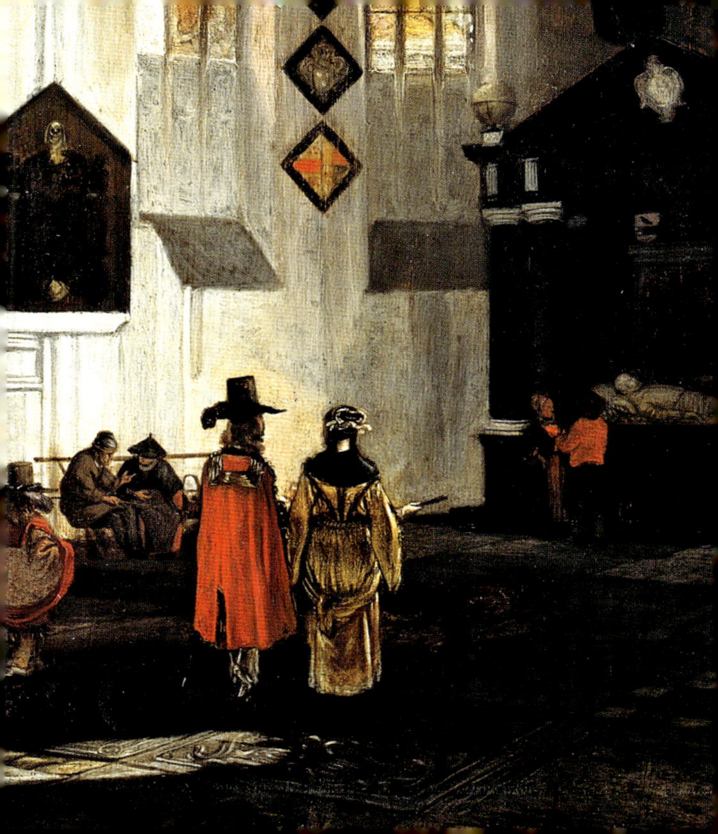

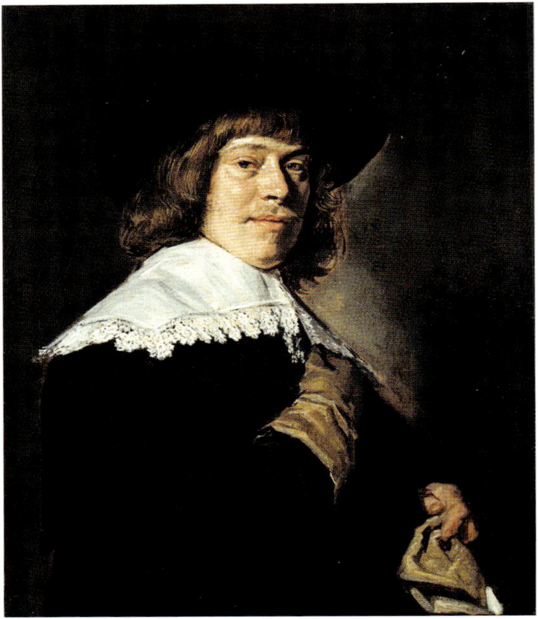

Frans Hals
Portrait of a Young Man Holding a Glove
Circa 1650. Holland

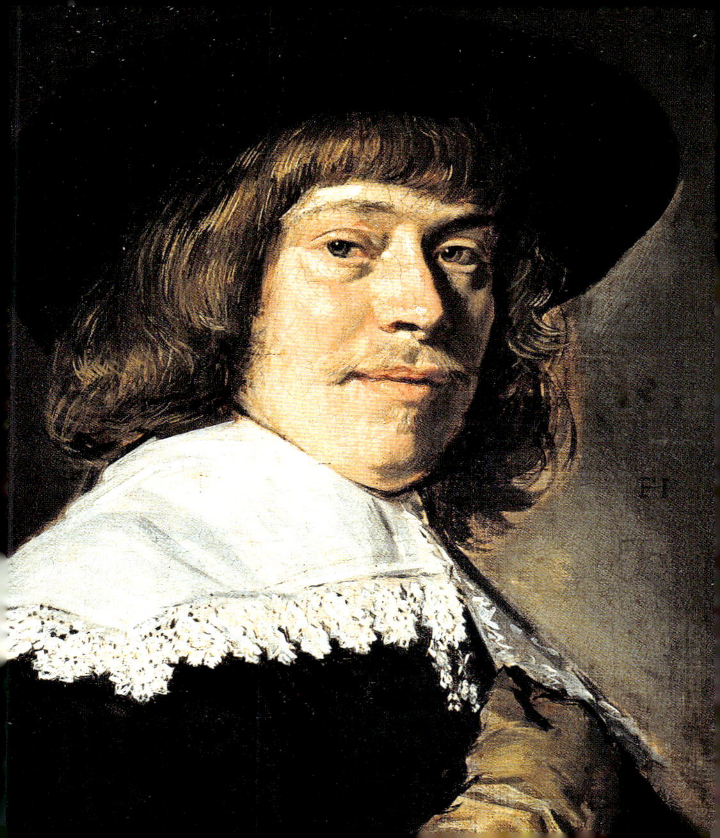
FH

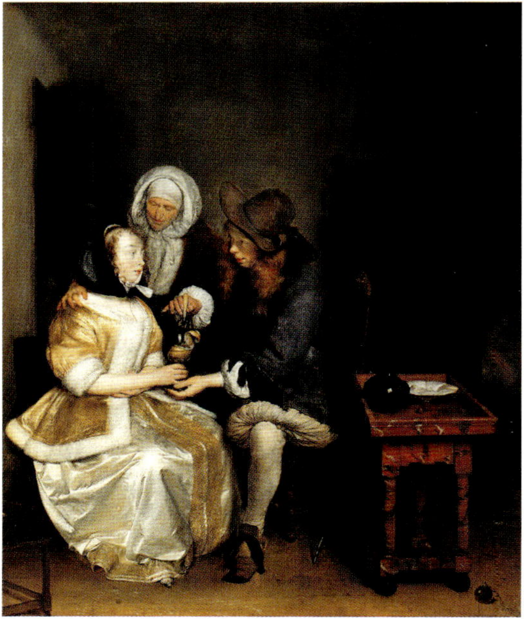

Gerard ter Borch
The Glass of Lemonade
1660s. Holland

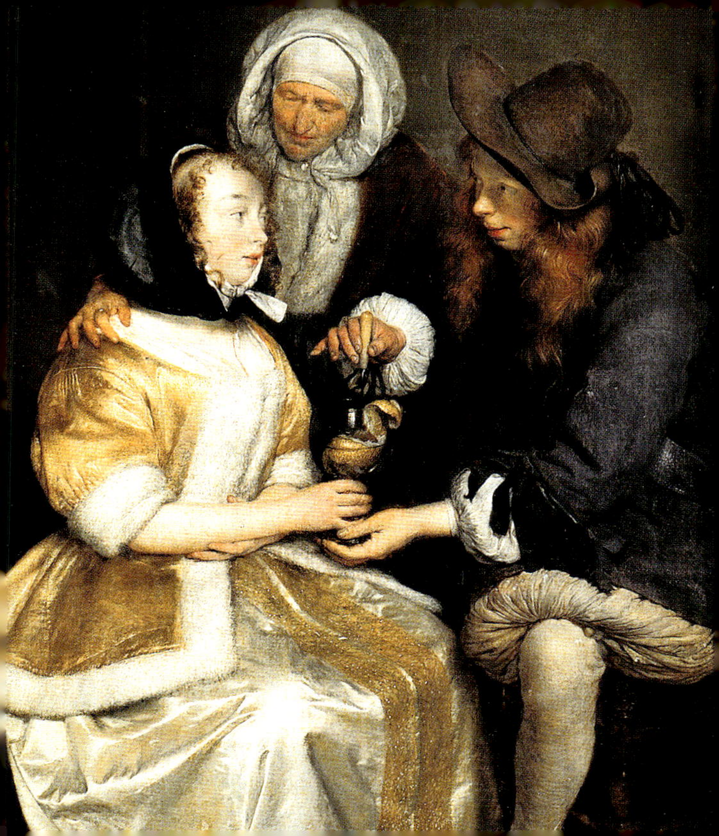

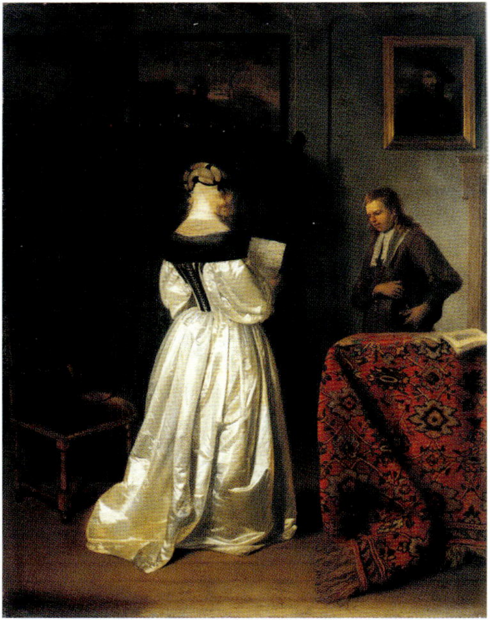

Gerard ter Borch
The Messenger
Early 17th century. Holland

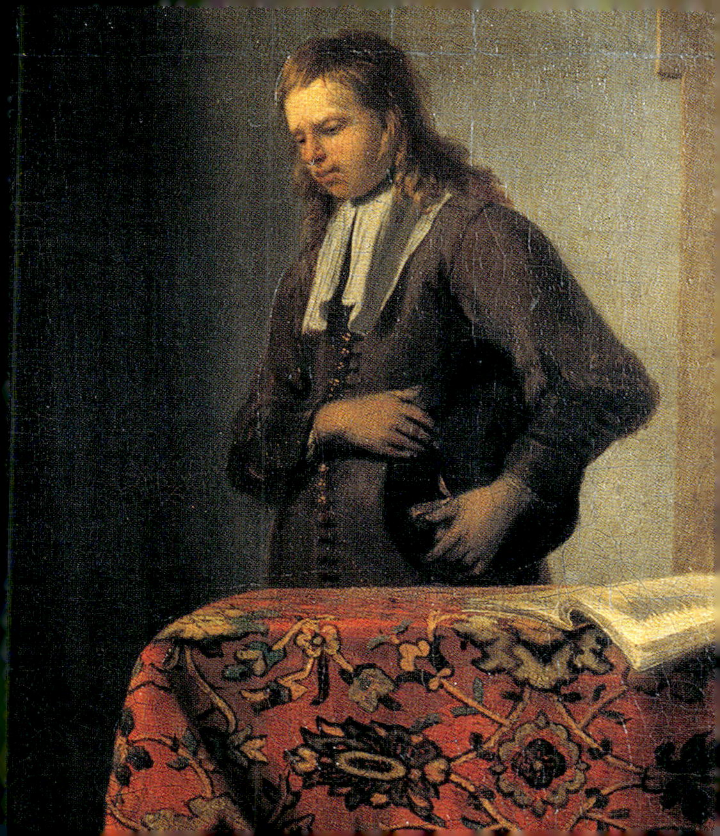

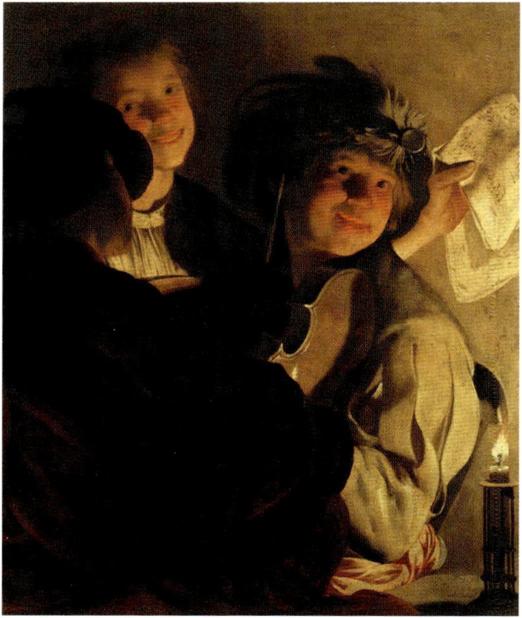

Hendrick Jansz Terbrugghen
Concert
1626. Holland

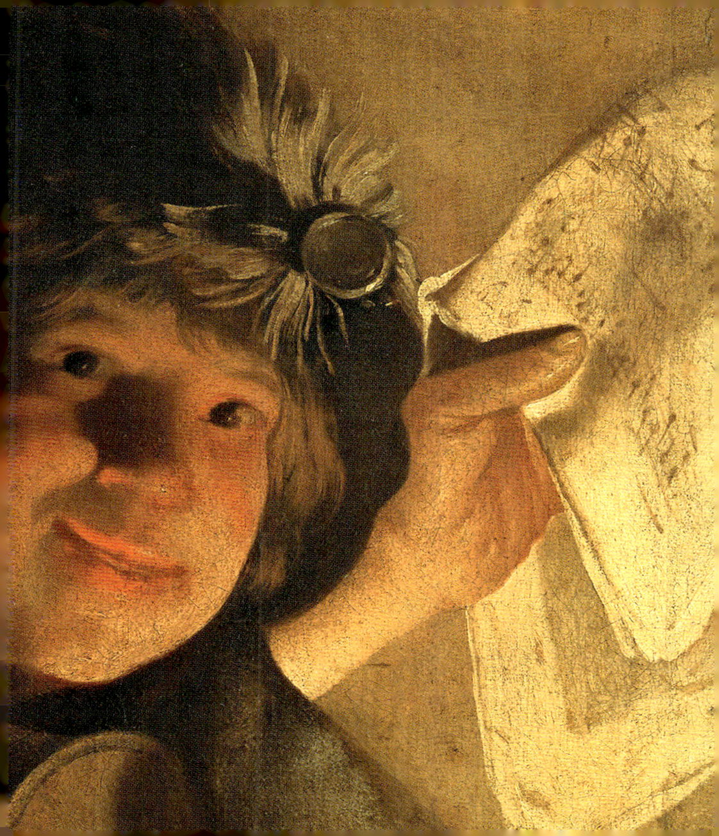

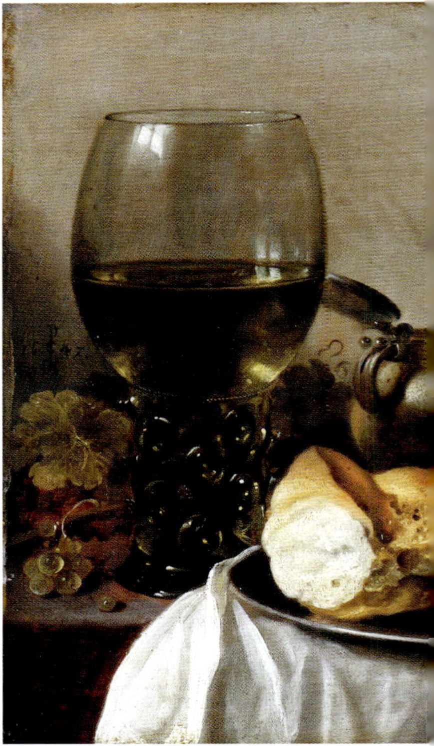

Pieter Claesz
Breakfast with Ham
1647. Holland

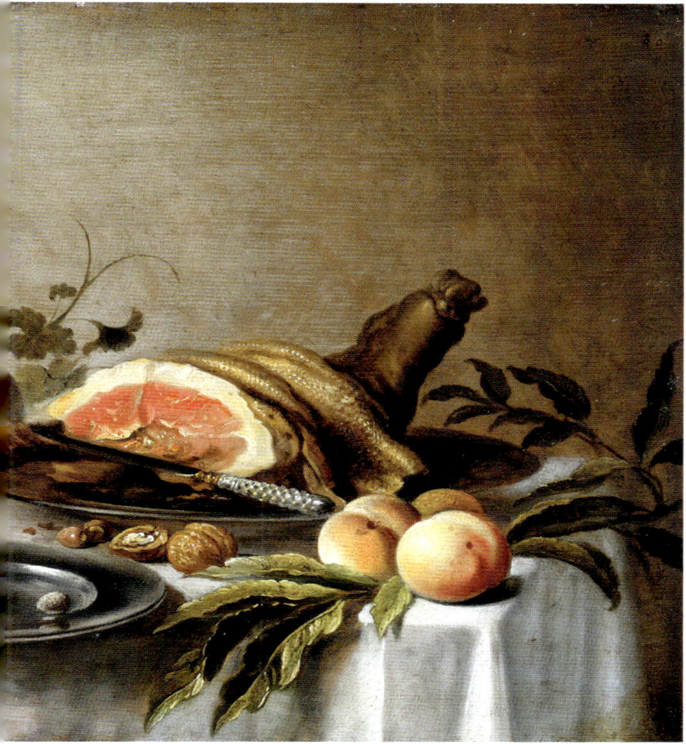

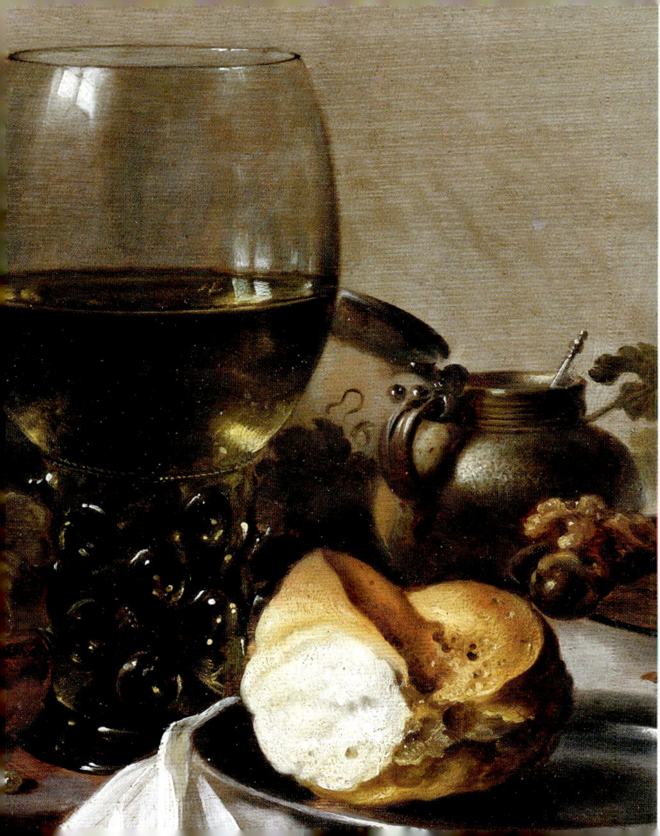

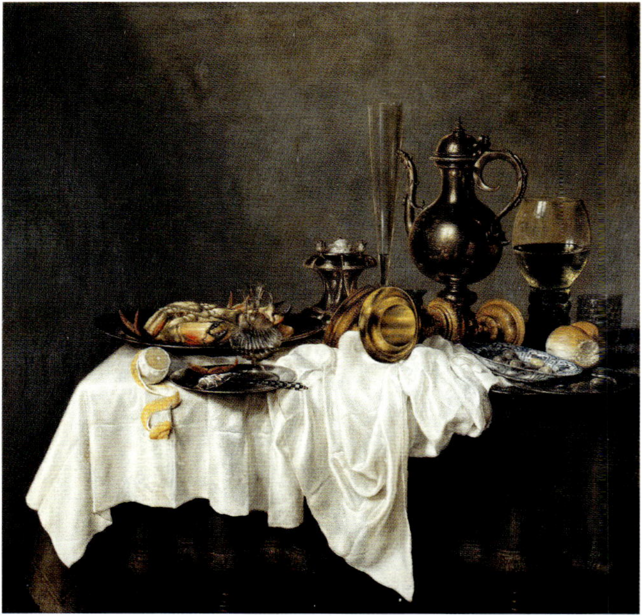

Willem Claesz Heda
Breakfast with a Lobster
1648. Holland

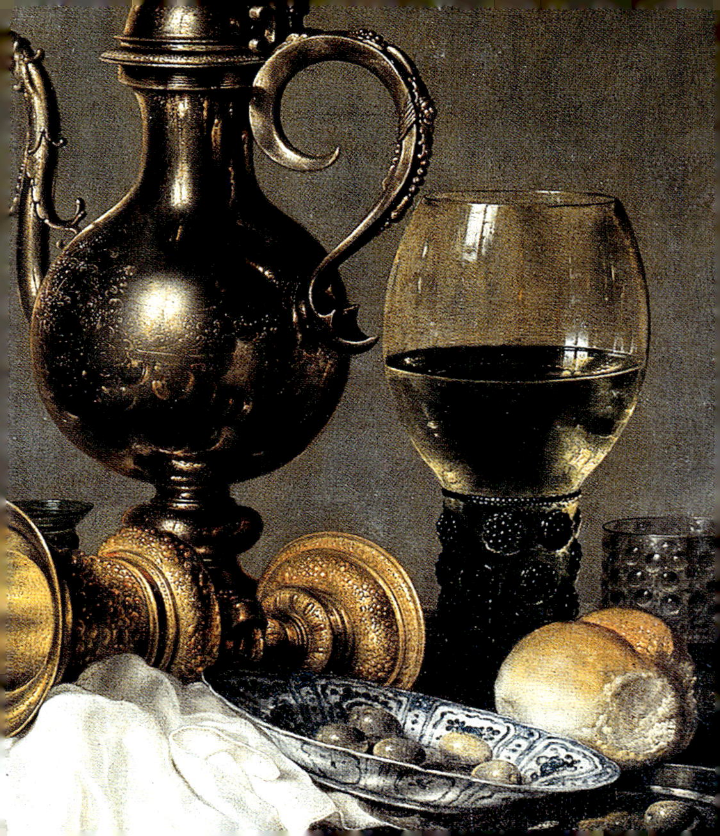

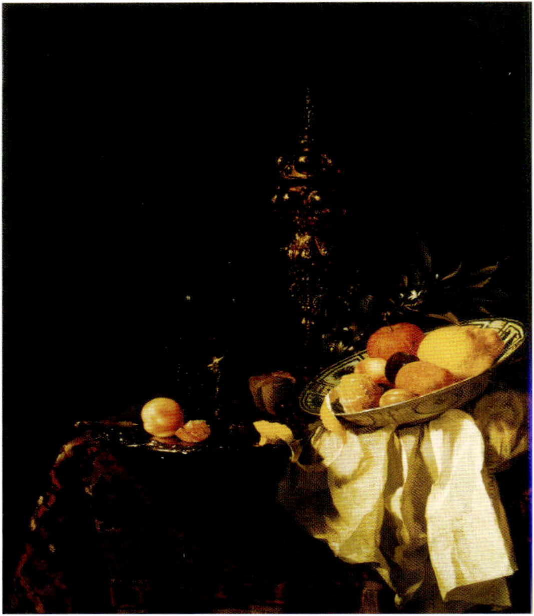

Willem Kalf
Dessert
1650s. Holland

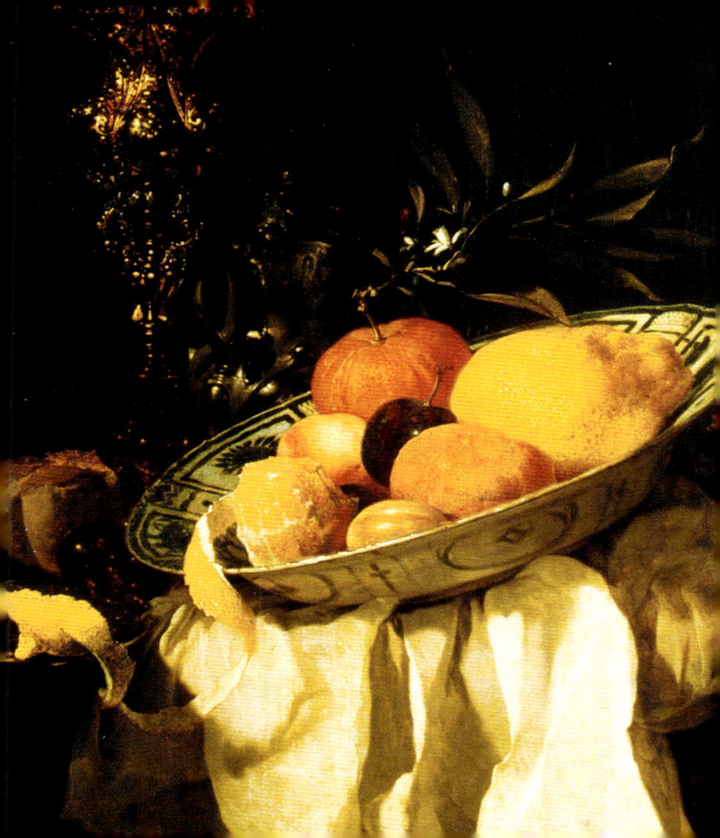

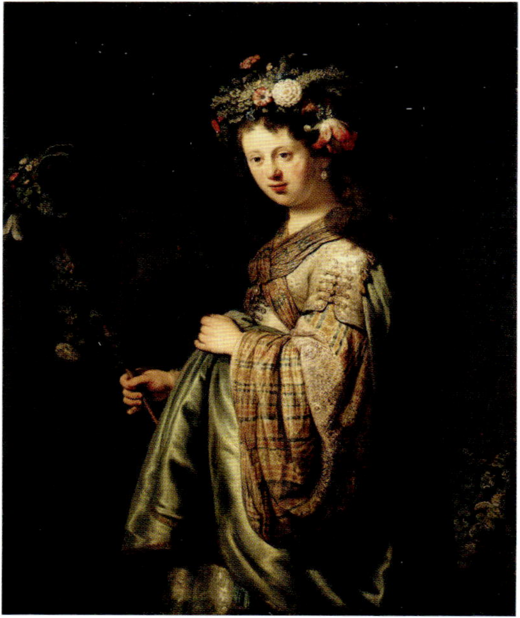

Rembrandt Harmensz van Rijn
Flora
1634. Holland

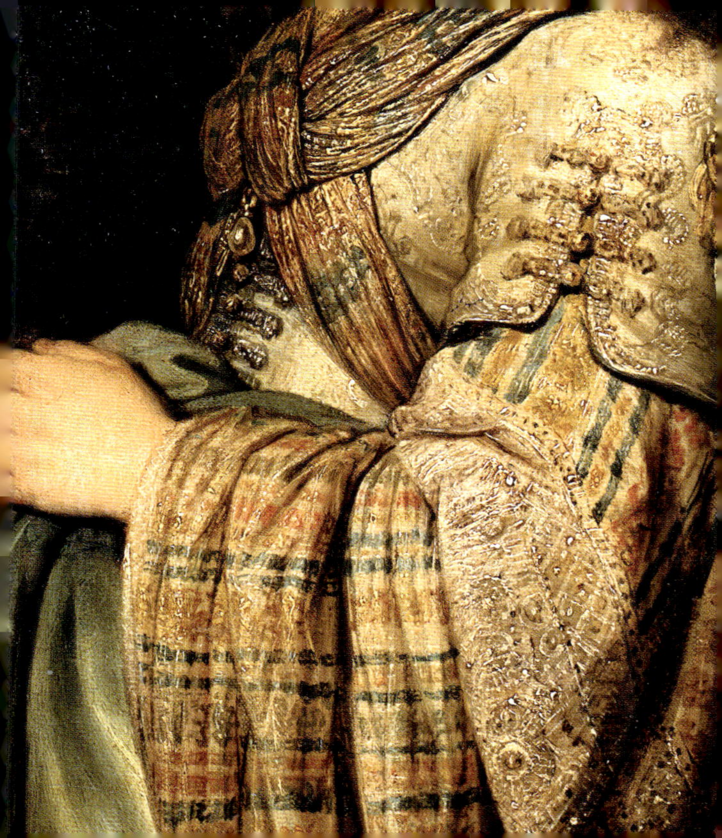

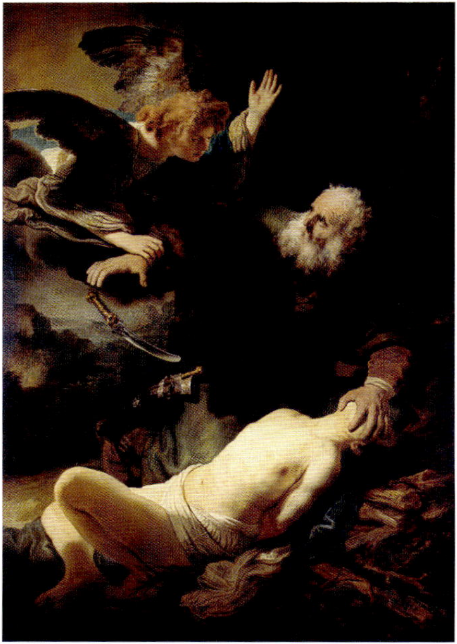

Rembrandt Harmensz van Rijn

The Sacrifice of Isaac

1635. Holland

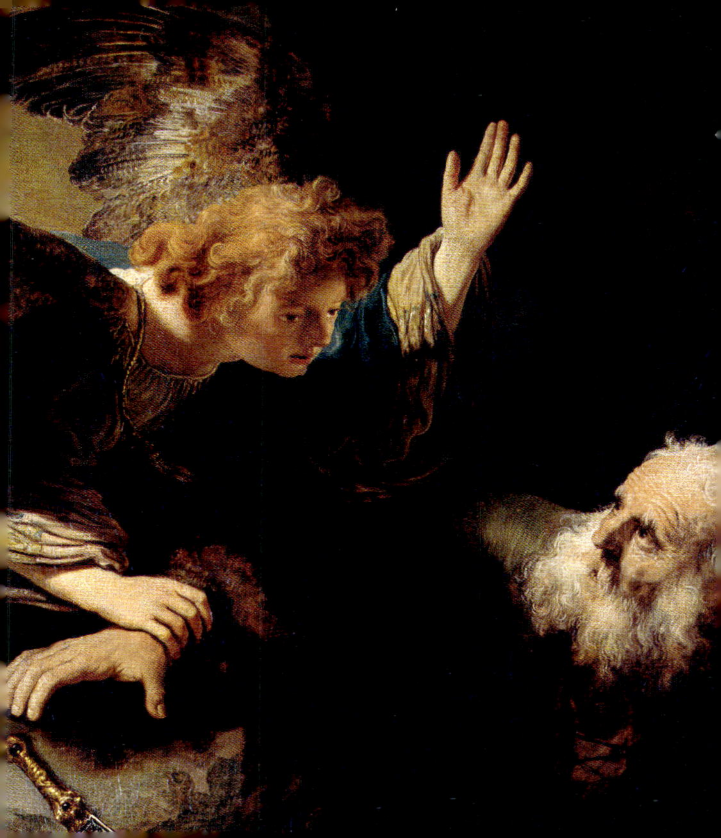

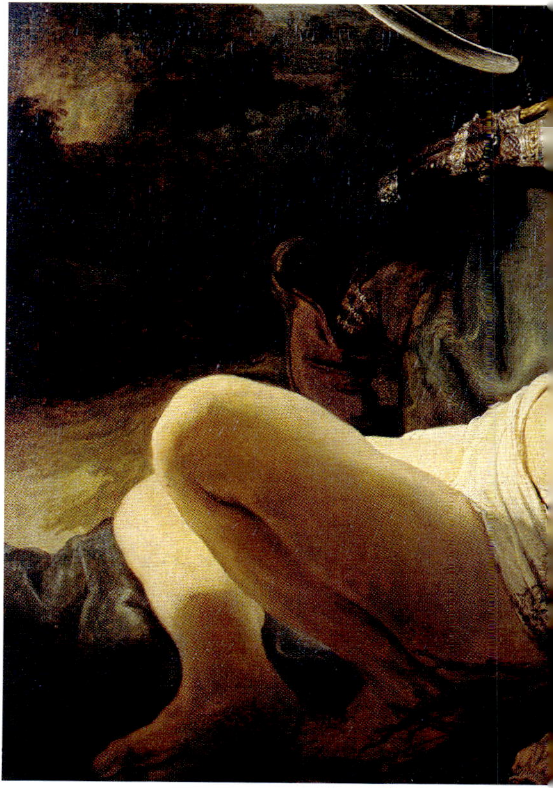

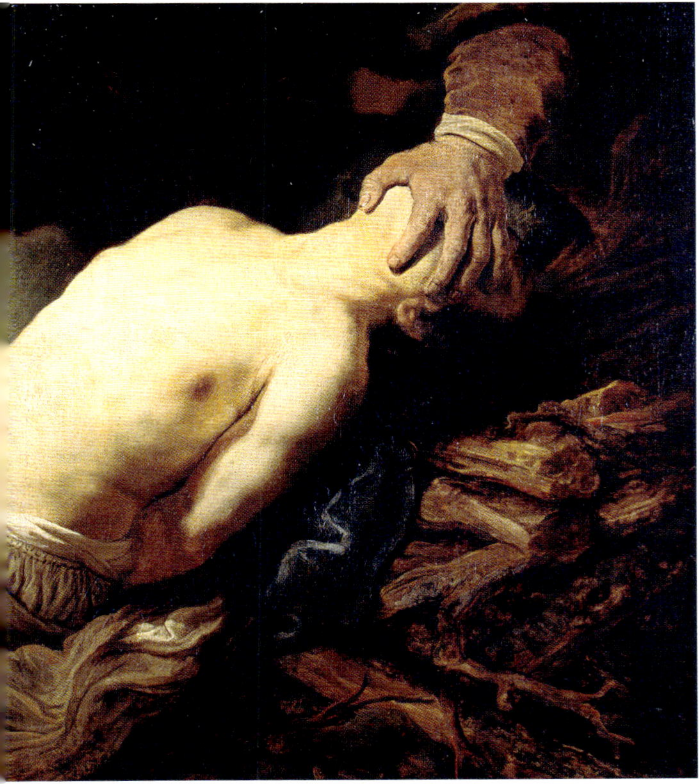

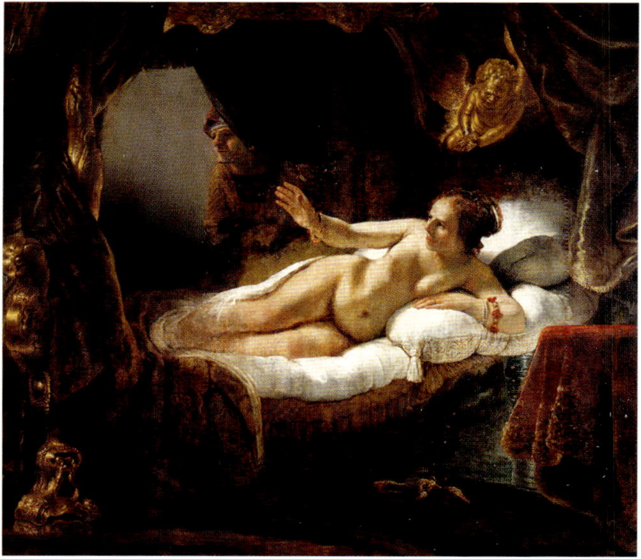

Rembrandt Harmensz van Rijn
Danae
1636. Holland

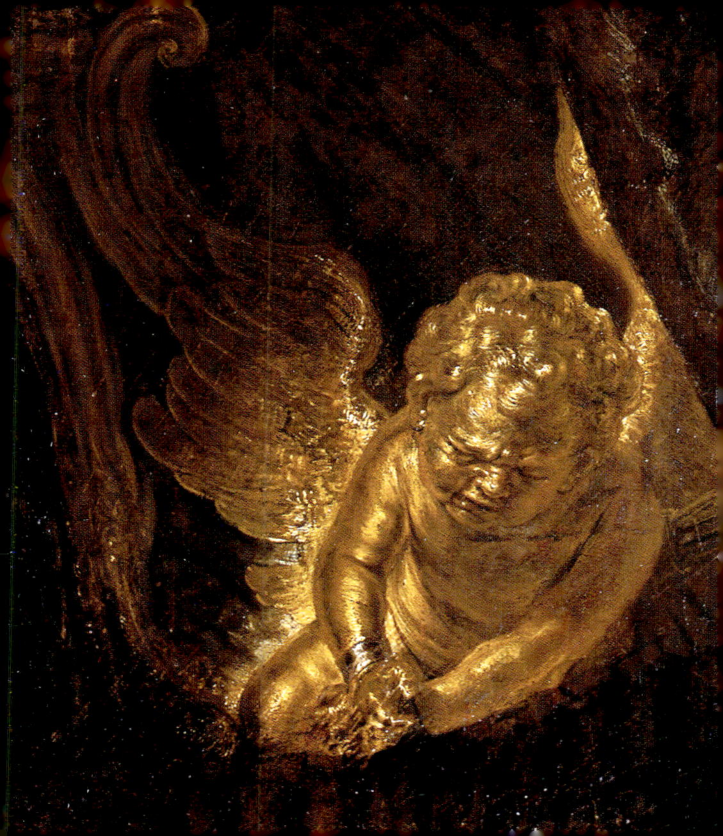

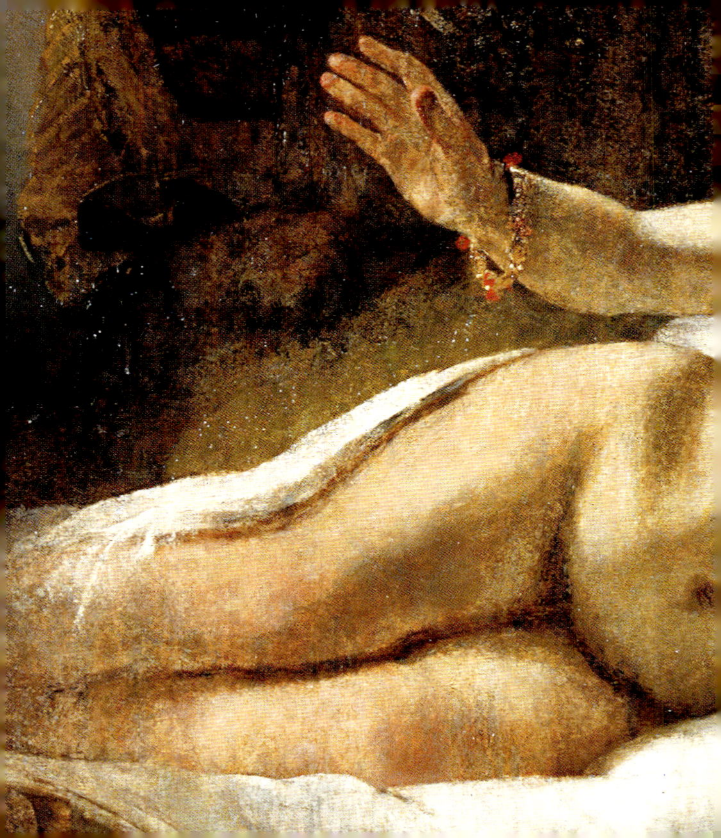

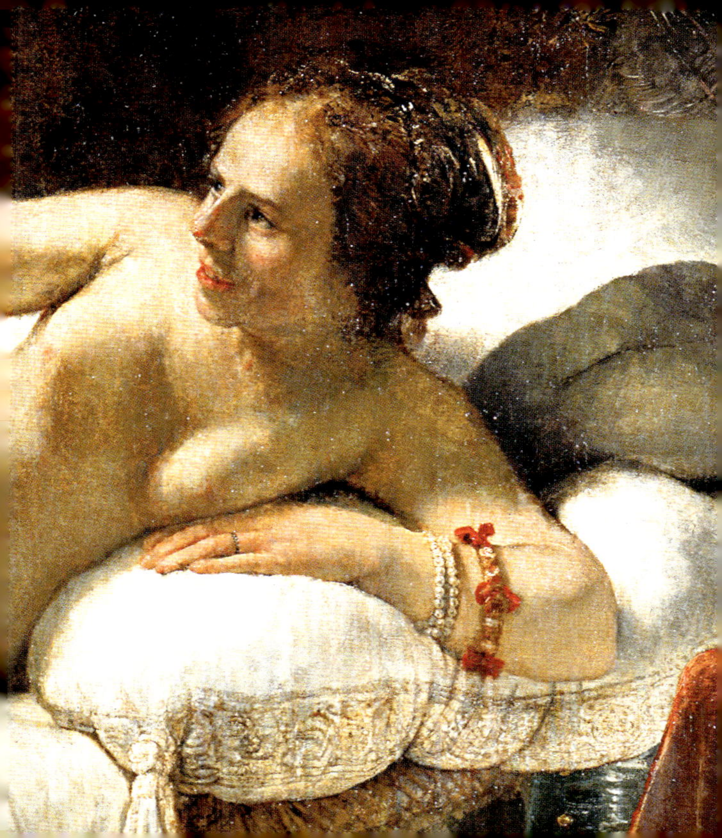

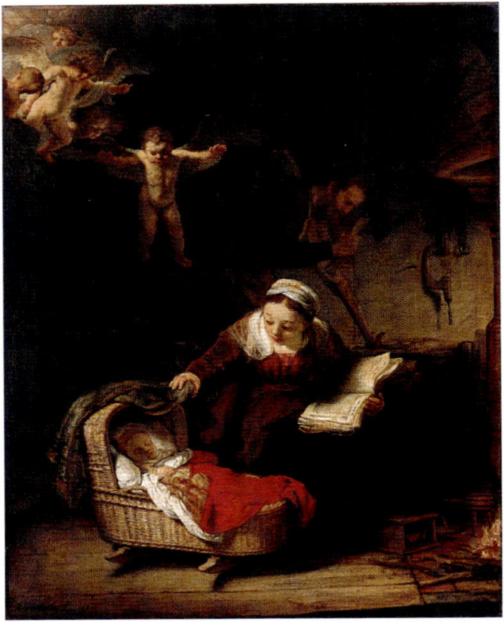

Rembrandt Harmensz van Rijn
The Holy Family
1645. Holland

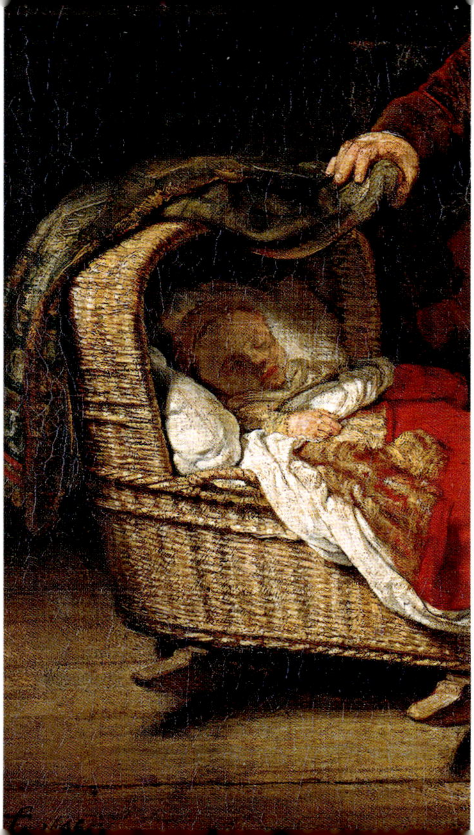

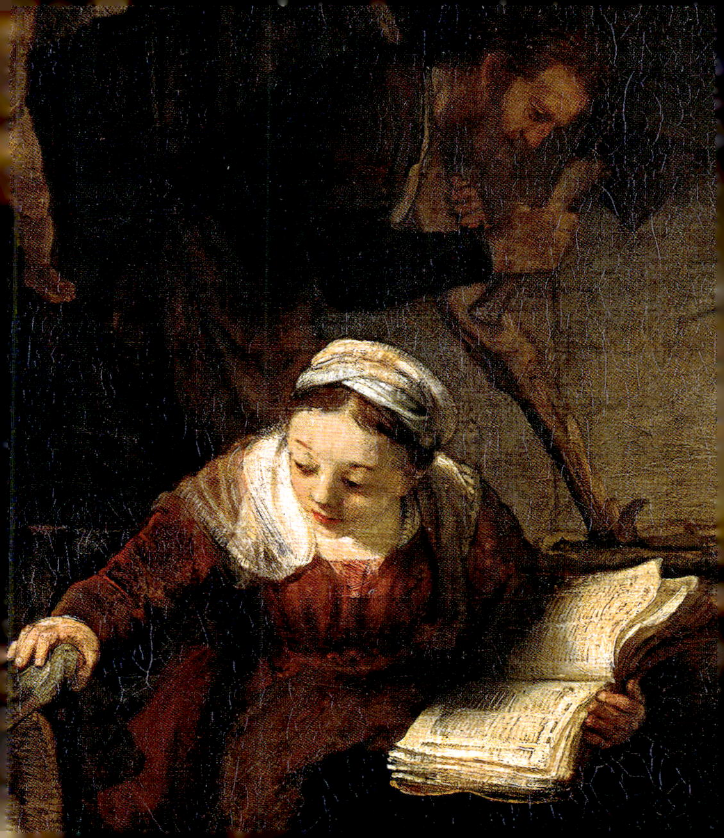

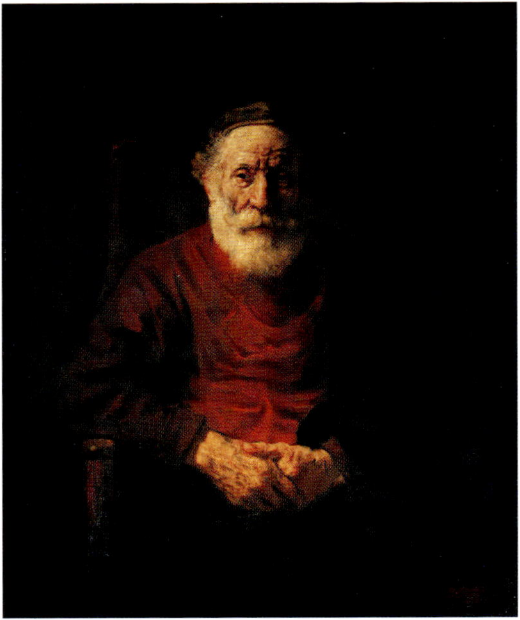

Rembrandt Harmensz van Rijn
Portrait of an Old Man in Red
Circa 1652–54. Holland

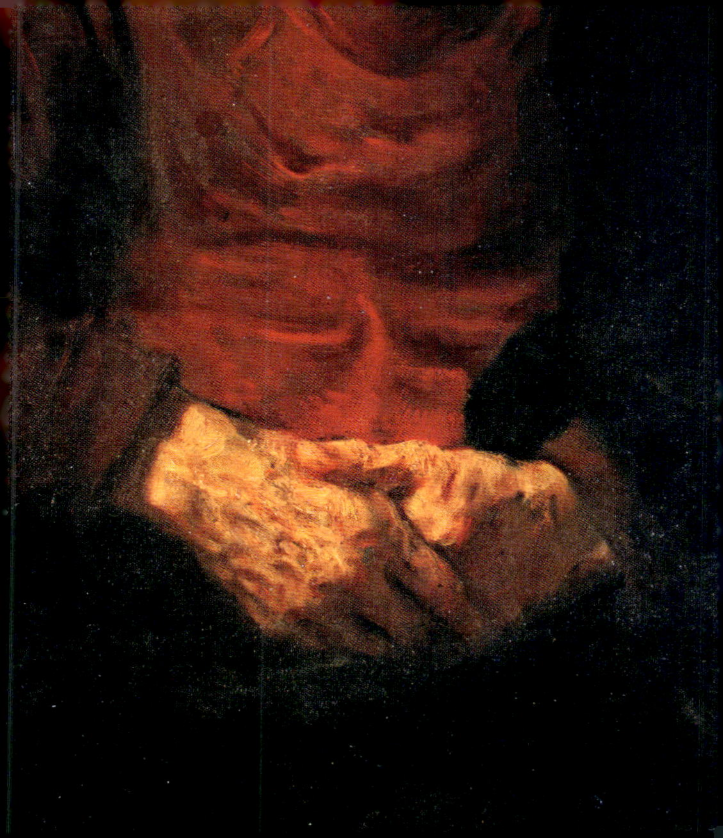

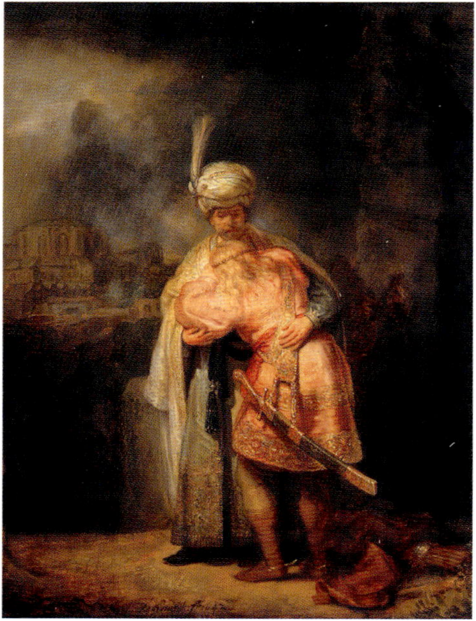

Rembrandt Harmensz van Rijn
David Parting with Jonathan
1642. Holland

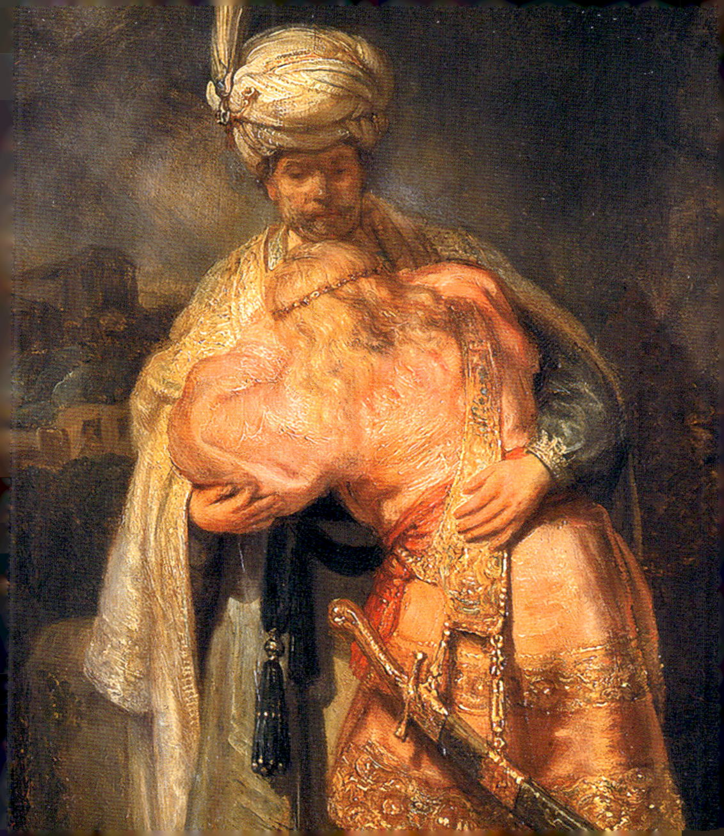

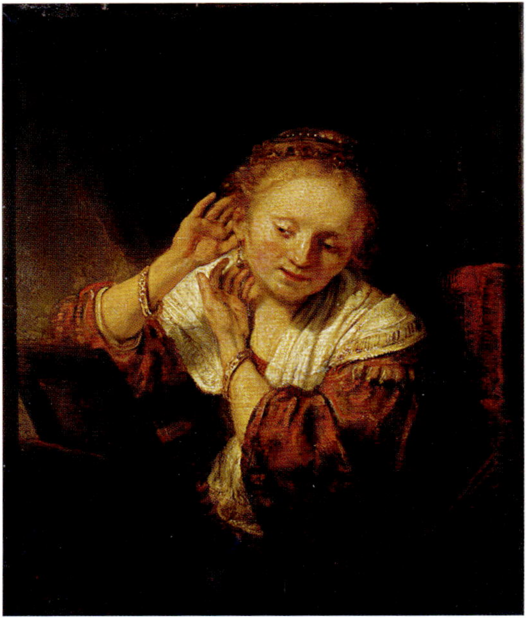

Rembrandt Harmensz van Rijn
Young Woman with Earrings
1657. Holland

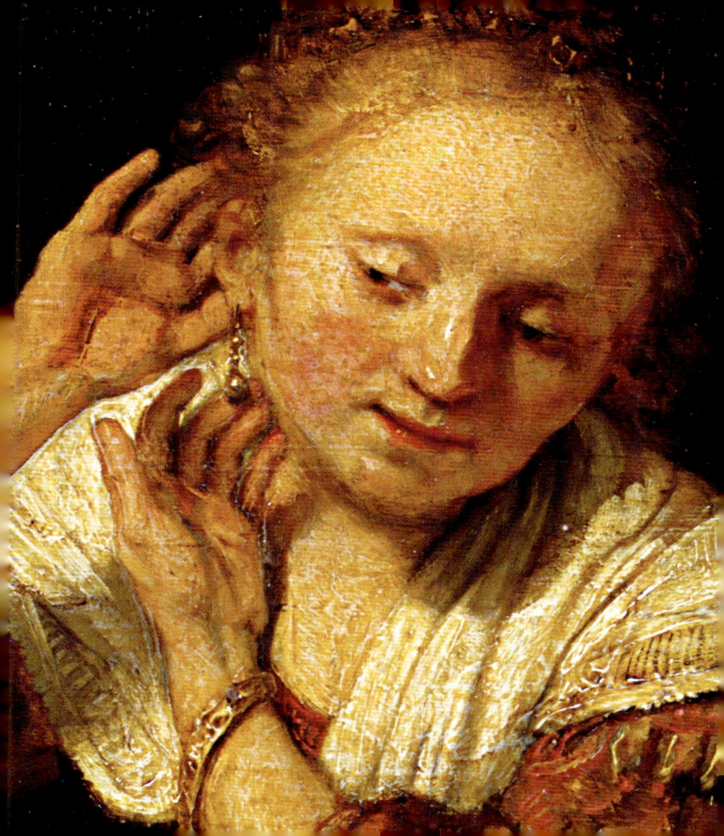

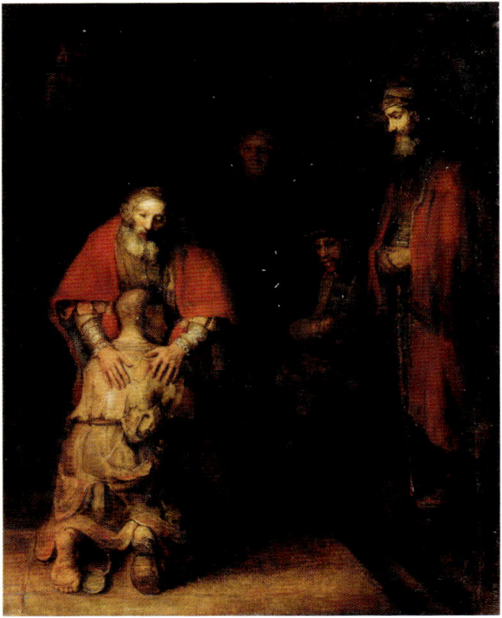

Rembrandt Harmensz van Rijn
The Return of the Prodigal Son
Circa 1668. Holland

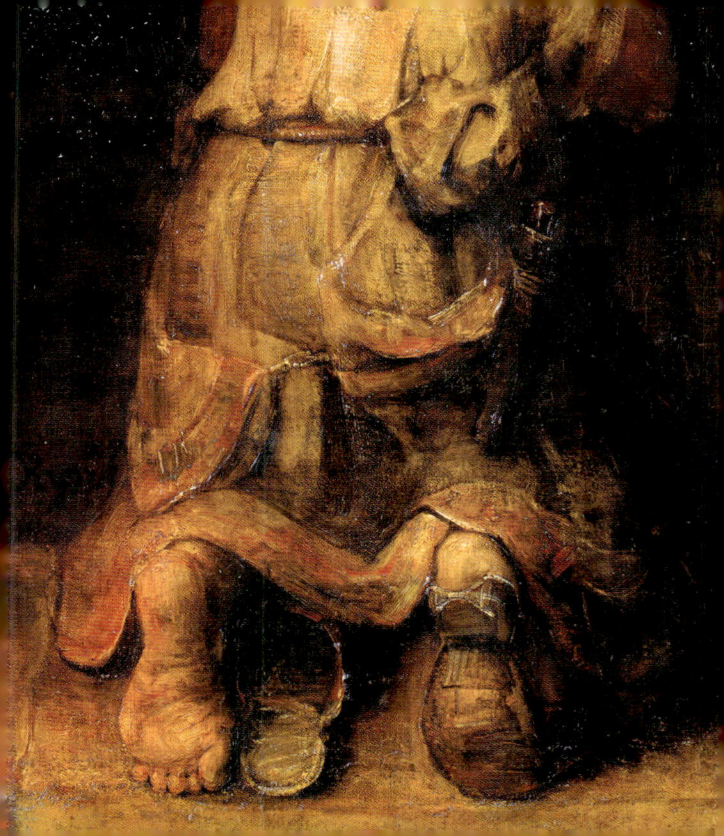

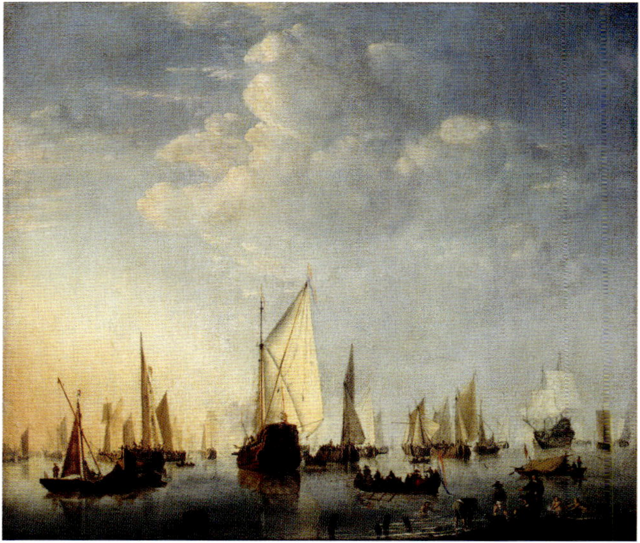

Willem van de Velde the Younger
Ships in a Calm Sea
1653. Holland

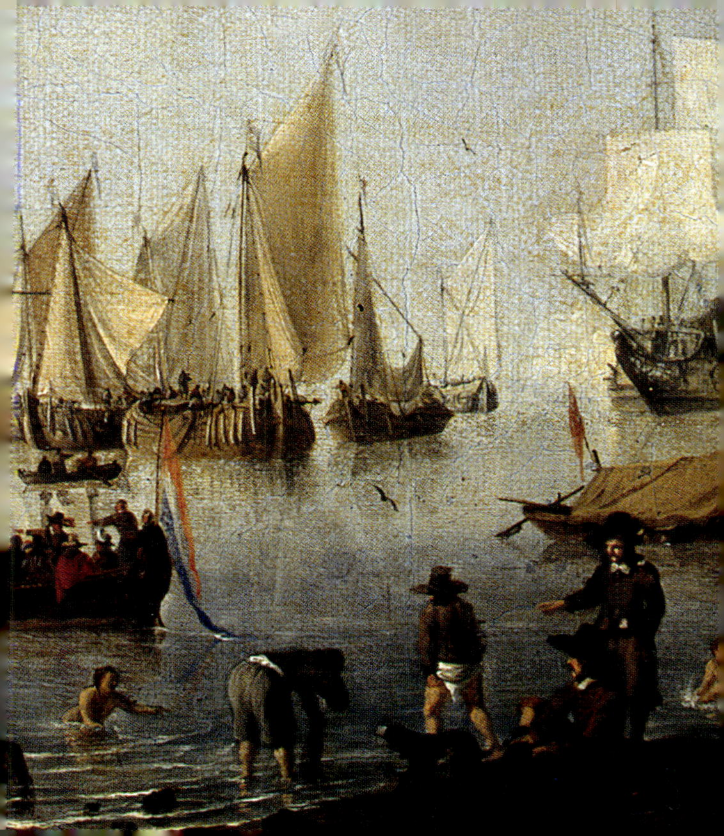

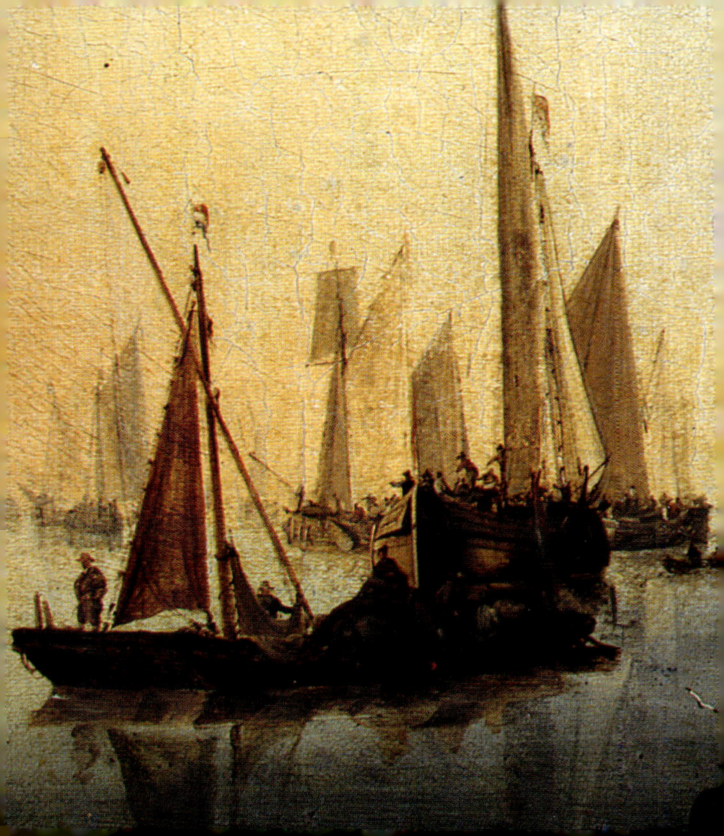

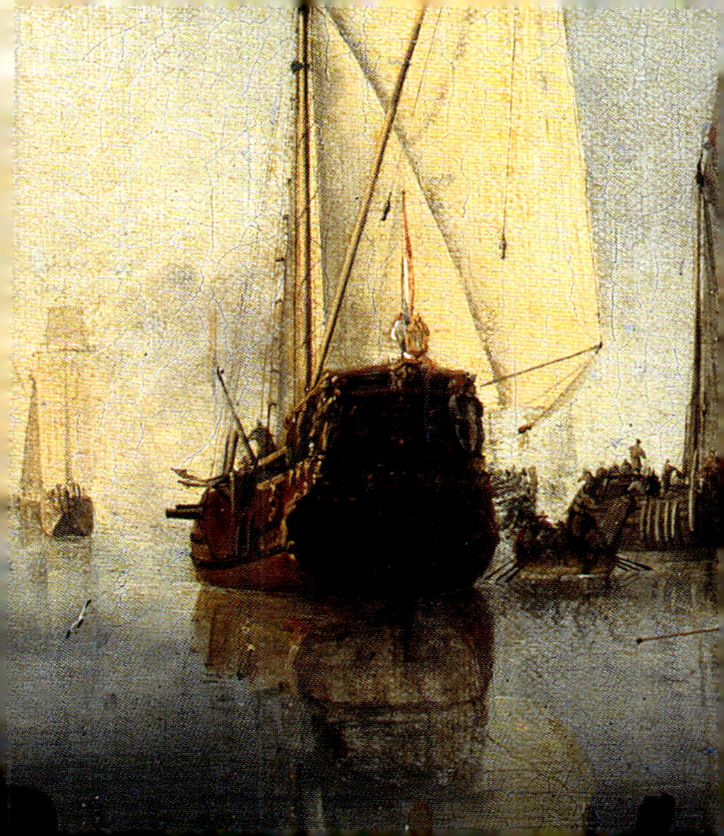

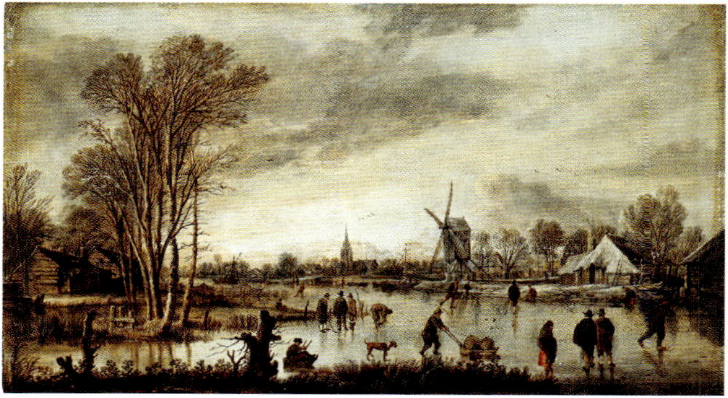

Aert van der Neer
A River in Winter
Circa 1645. Holland

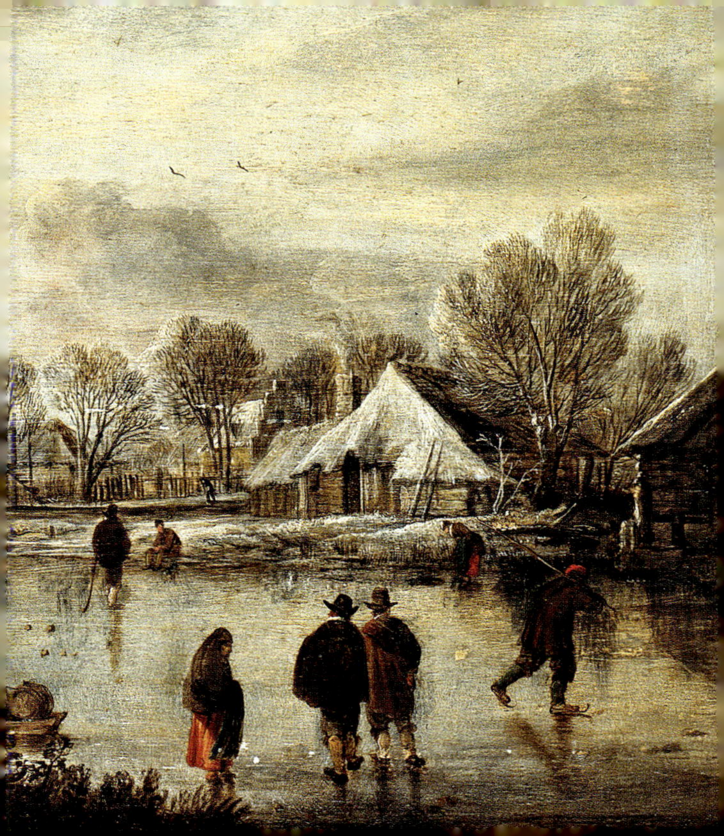

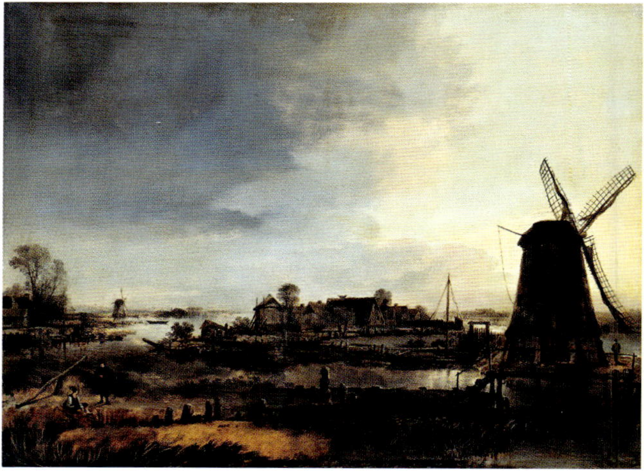

Aert van der Neer
Landscape with a Windmill
Circa 1646. Holland

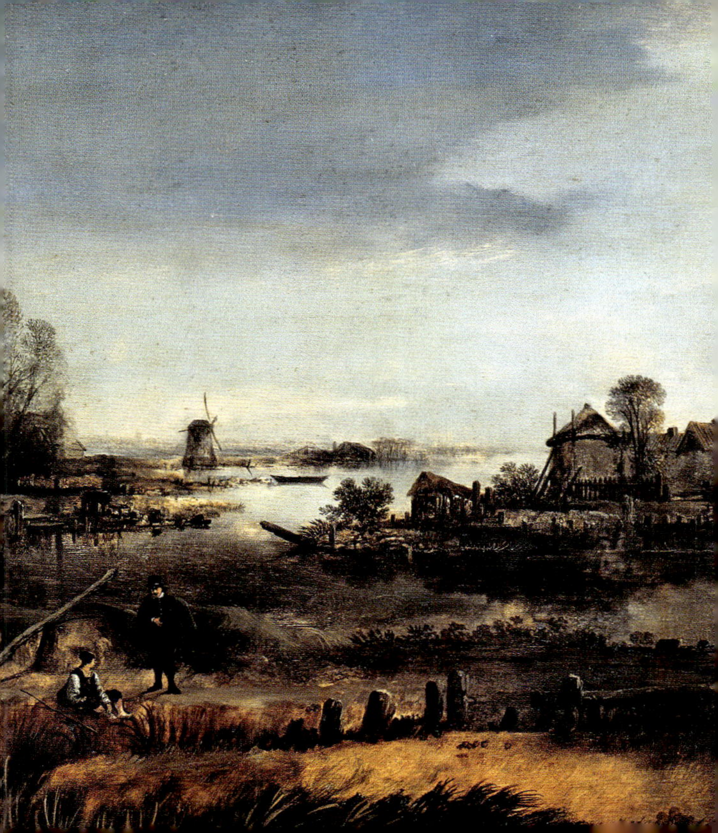

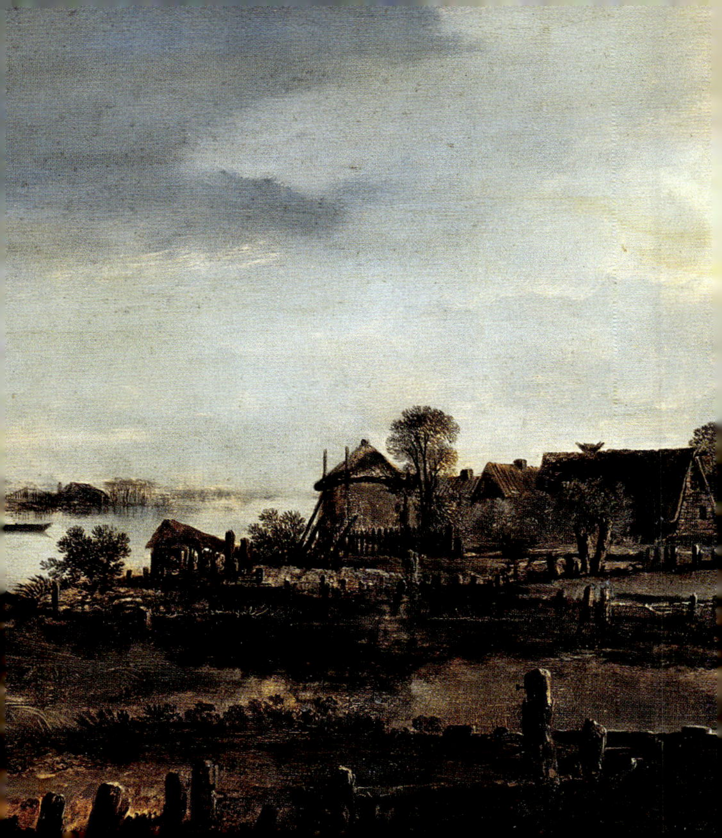

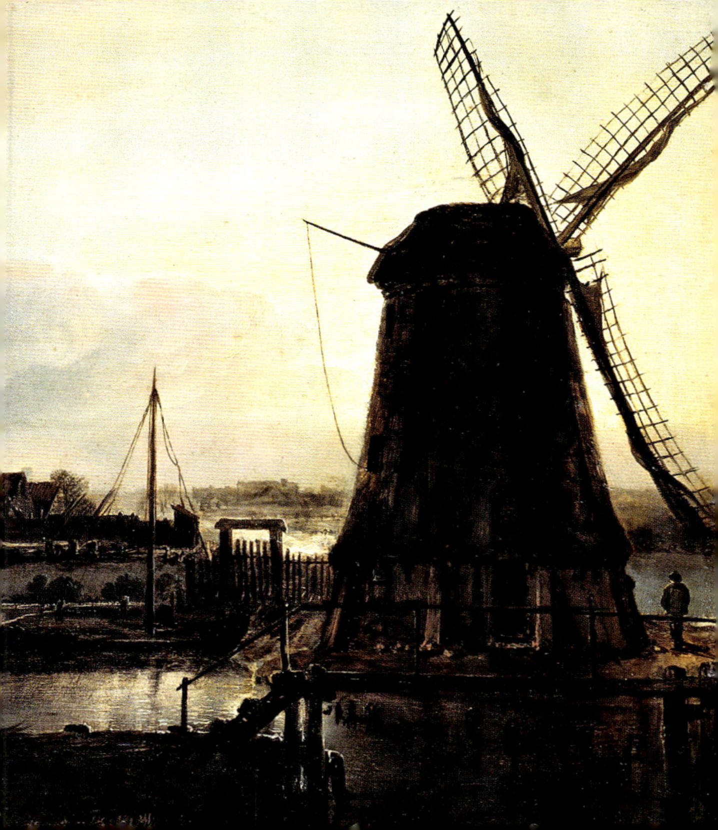

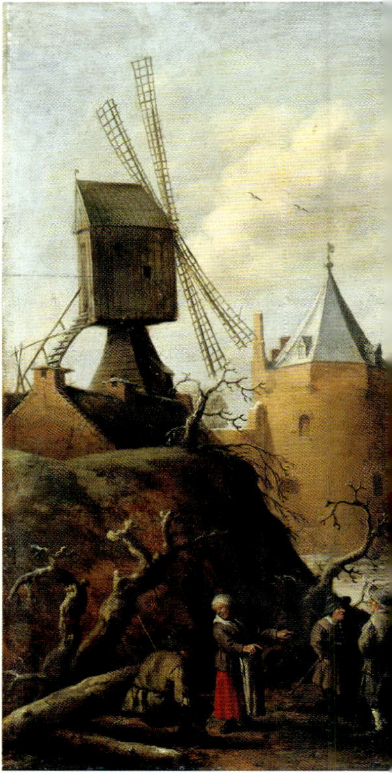

Joost Cornelisz Droochsloot
Winter in a Dutch Town
Early 17th century. Holland

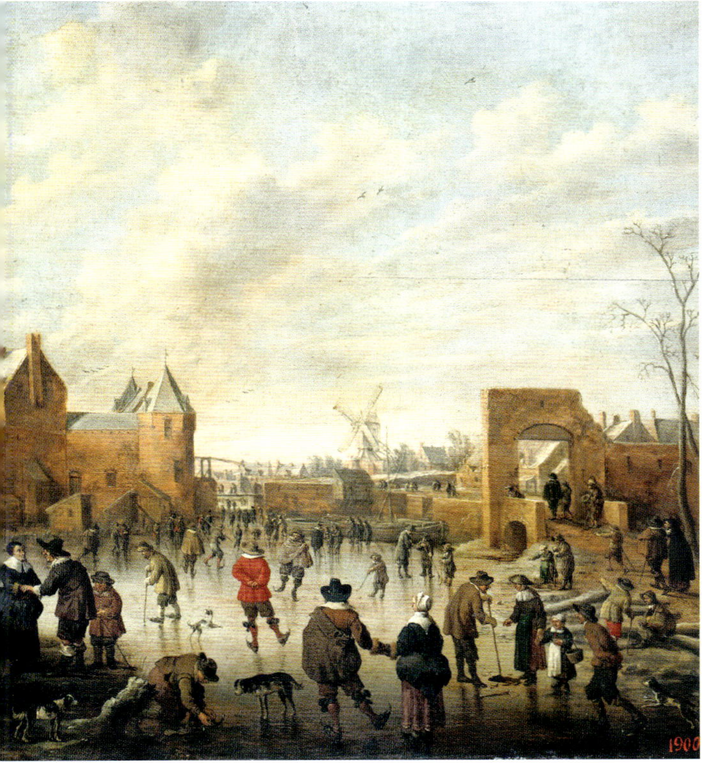
1900

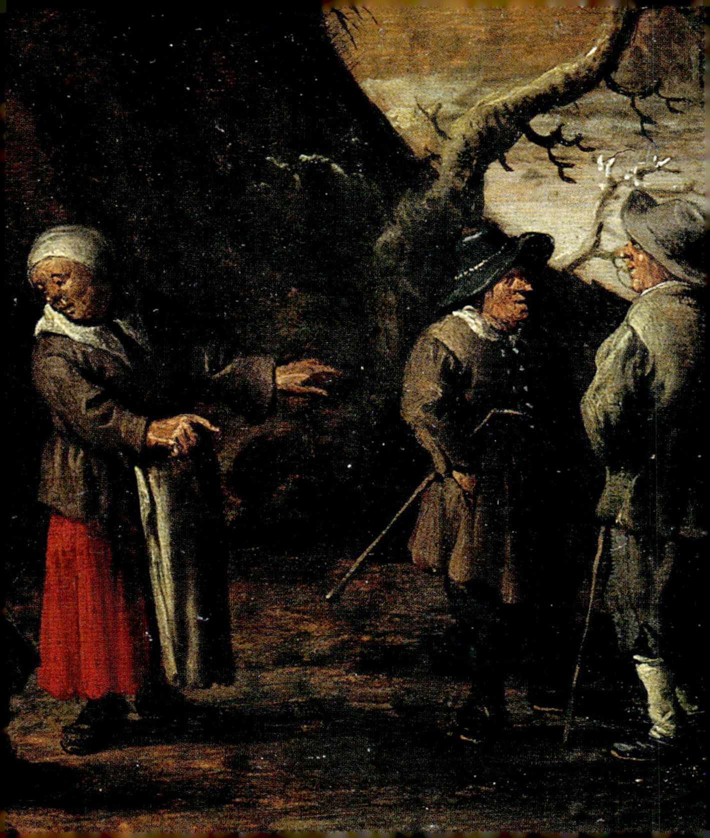

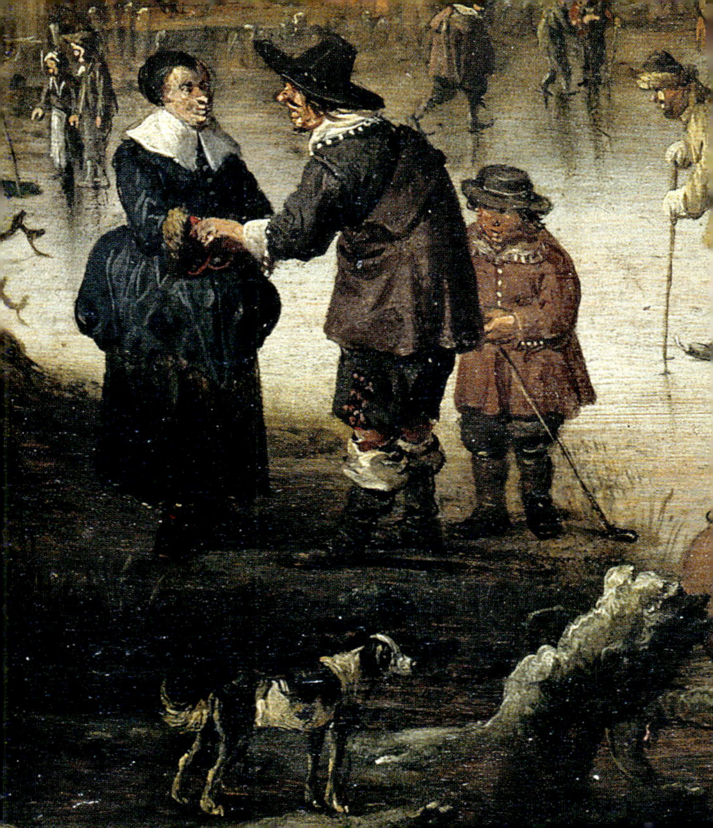

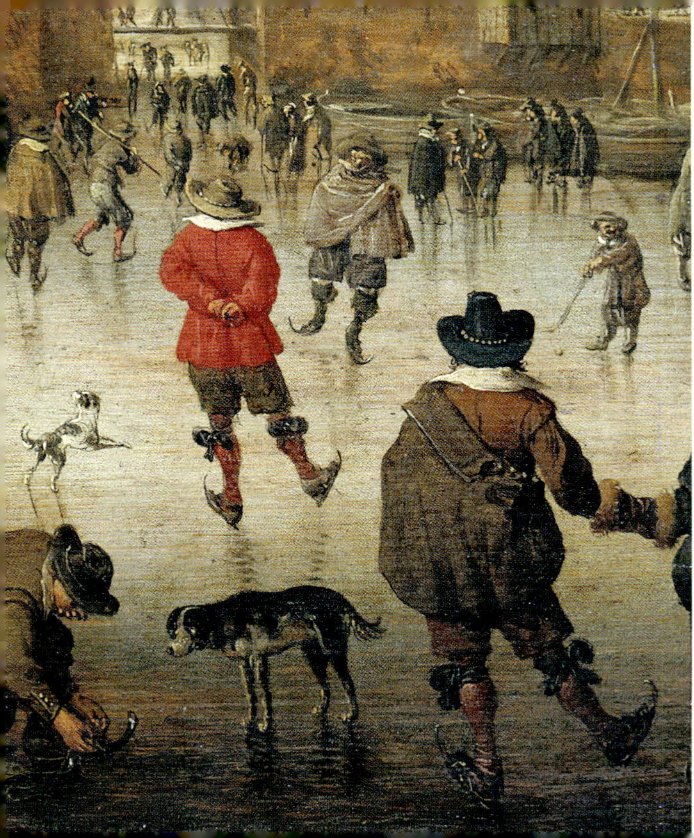

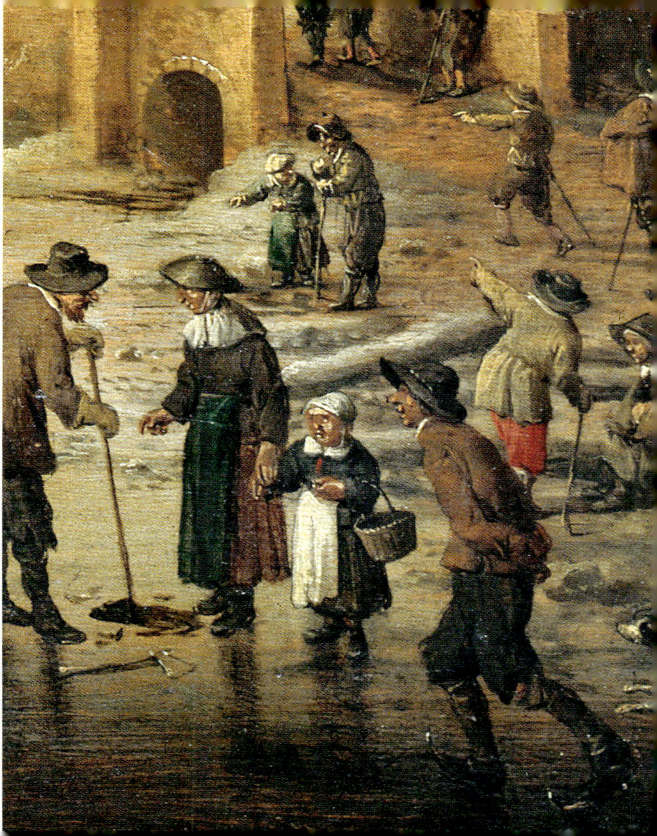

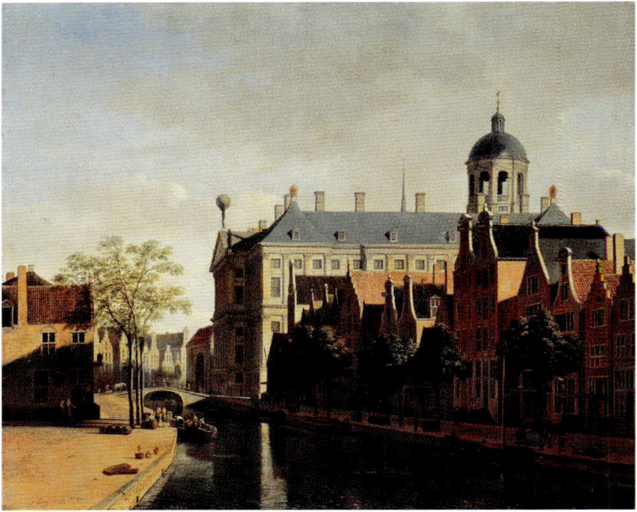

Gerrit Adriaensz Berckheyde
View of the Ratshuis in Amsterdam
Early 17th century. Holland

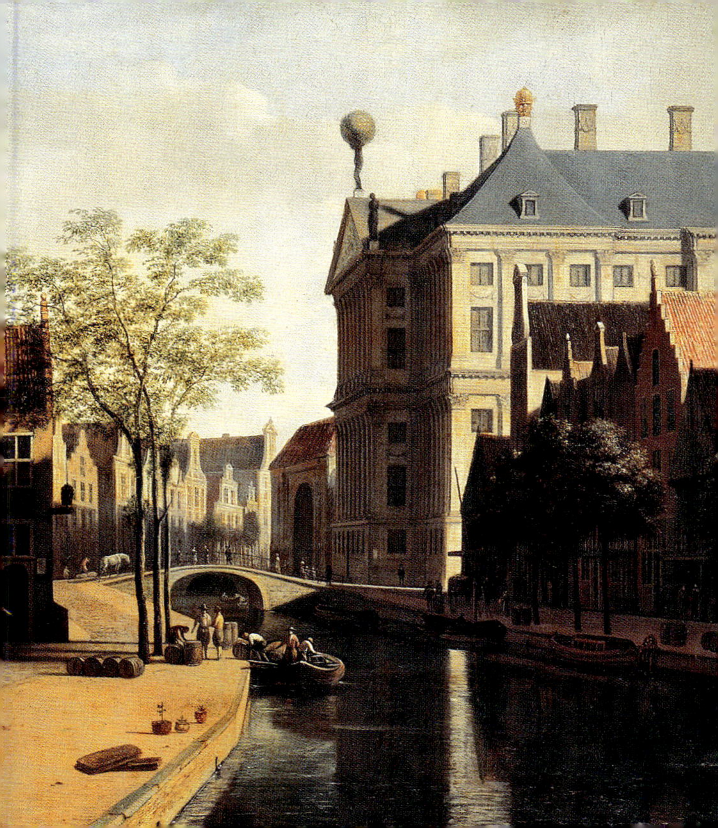

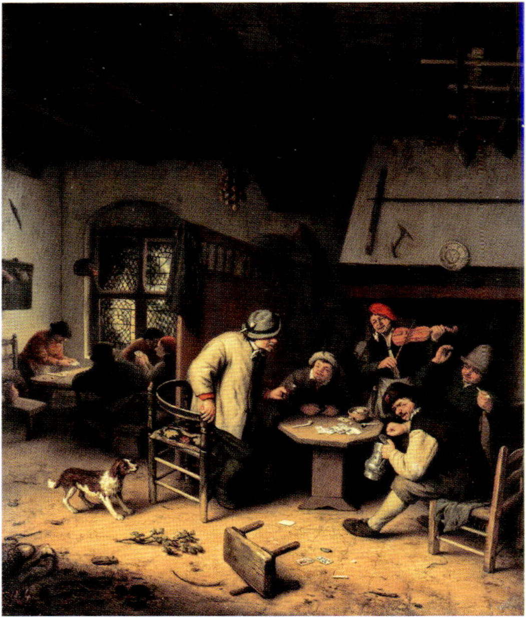

Adriaen van Ostade
Peasants in a Tavern
1671. Holland

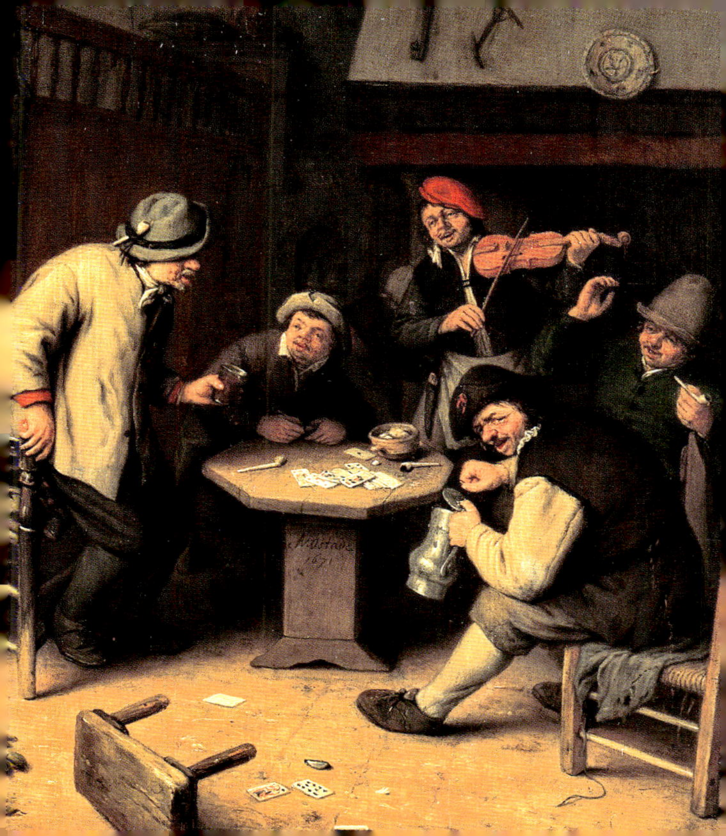

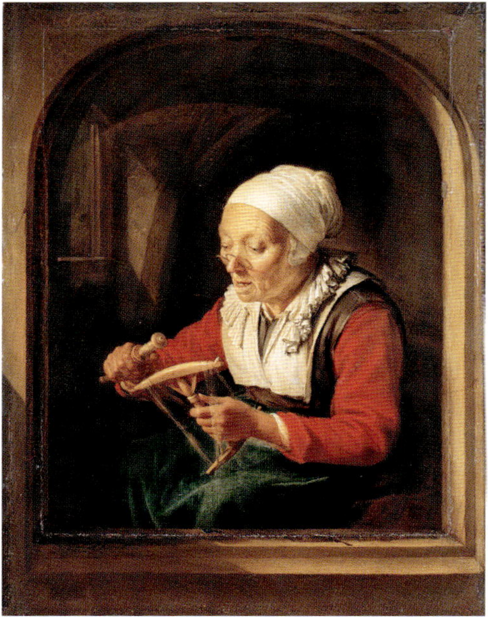

Gerard Dou
Old Woman Unreeling Threads
Circa 1660–5. Holland

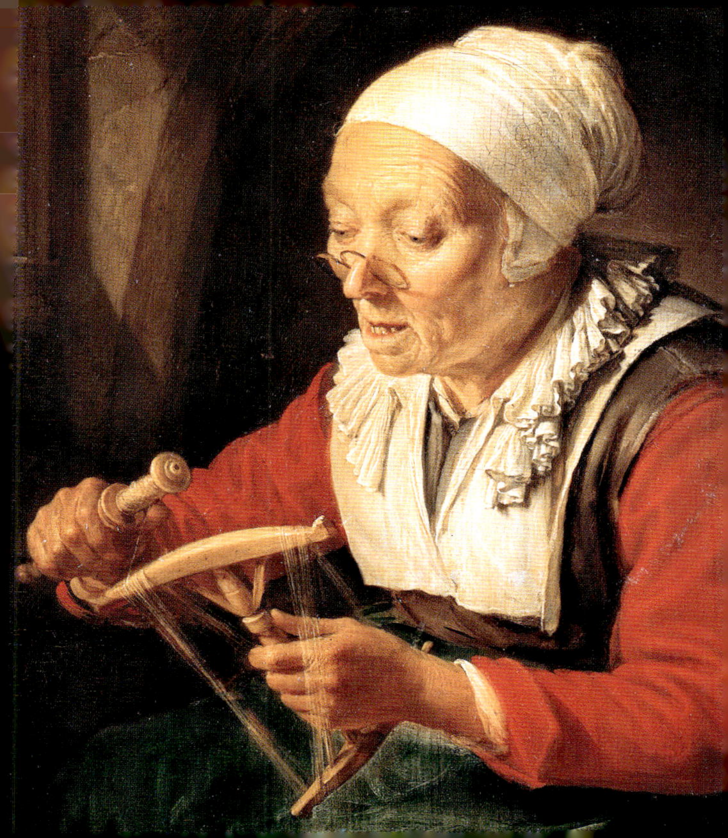

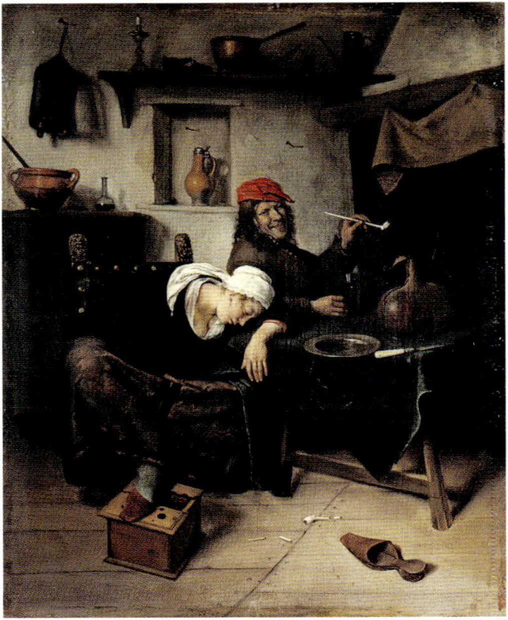

Jan Steen
The Idlers
Circa 1660. Holland

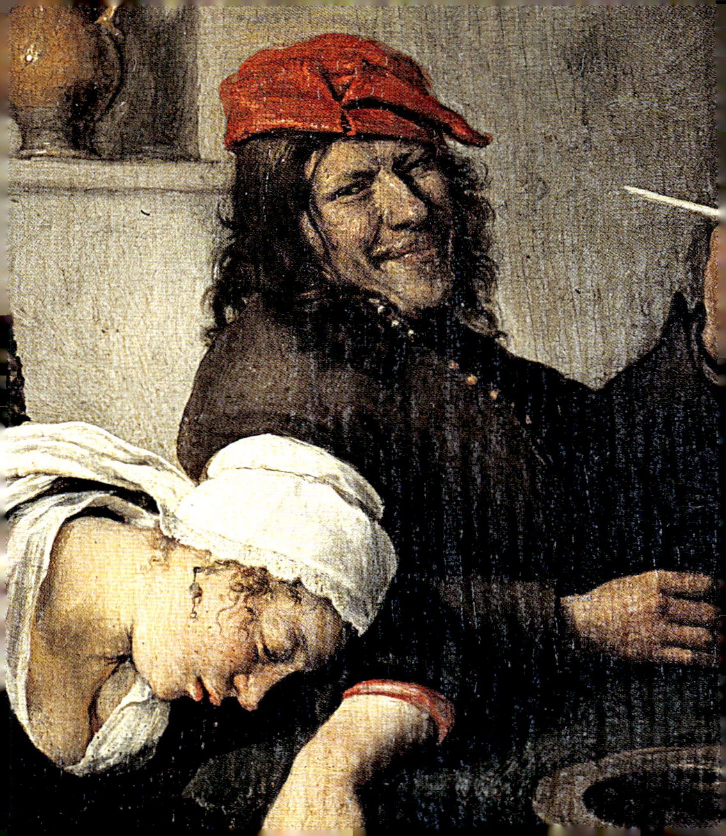

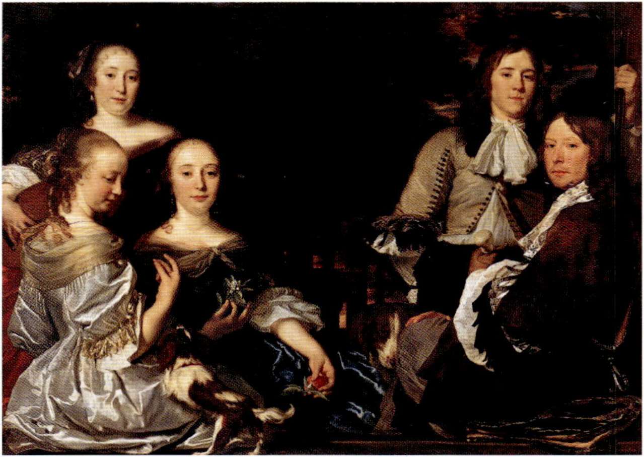

Abraham van den Tempel
Family Portrait
Early 17th century. Holland

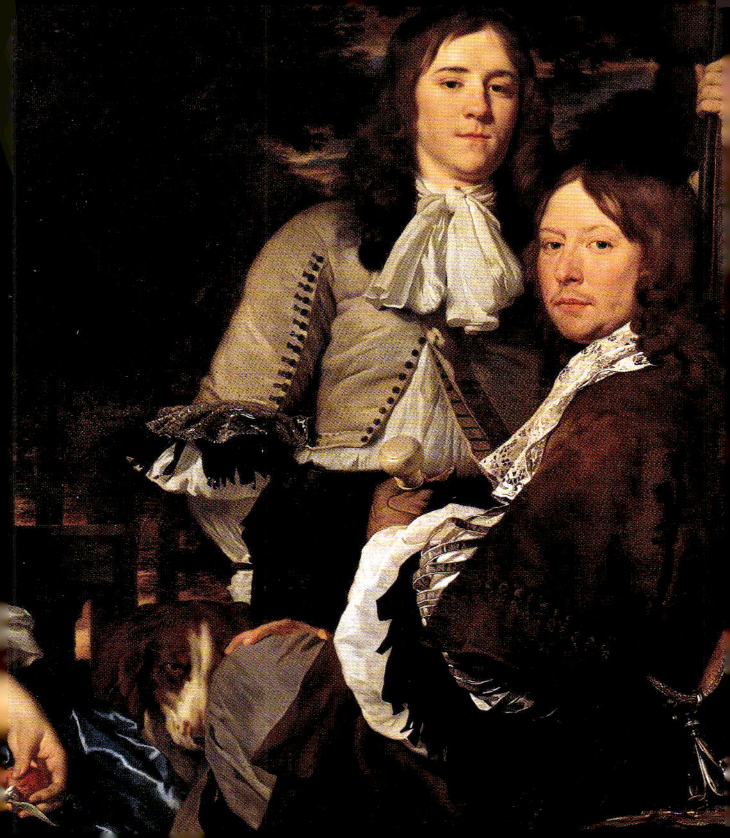

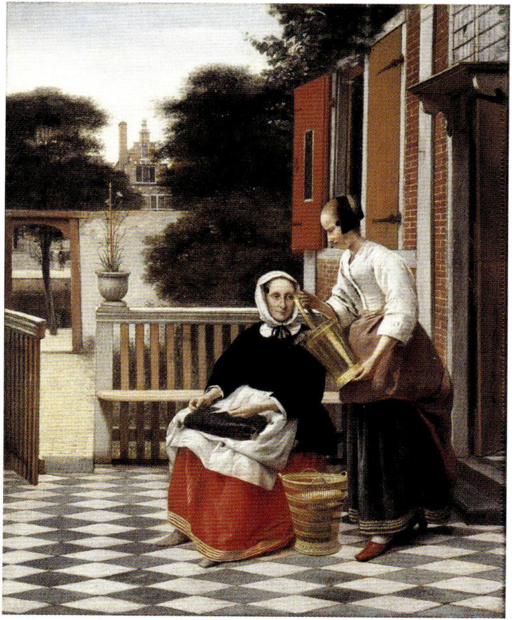

Pieter de Hooch
A Mistress and Her Maid
Circa 1660. Holland

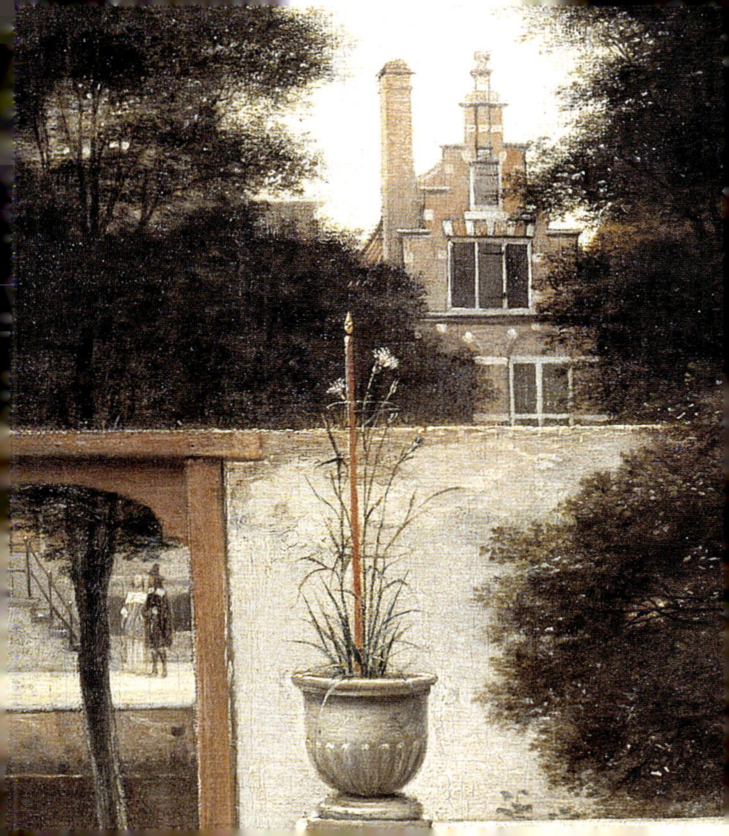

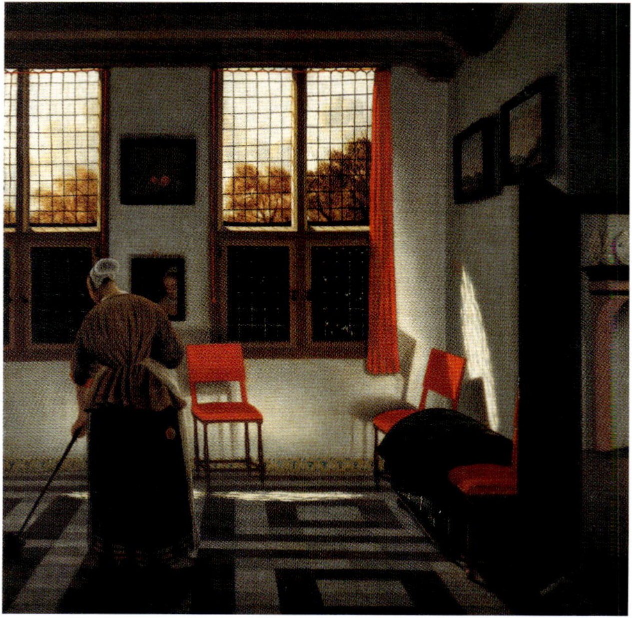

Pieter Janssens Elinga
A Room in a Dutch House
Late 1660s – early 1670s. Holland

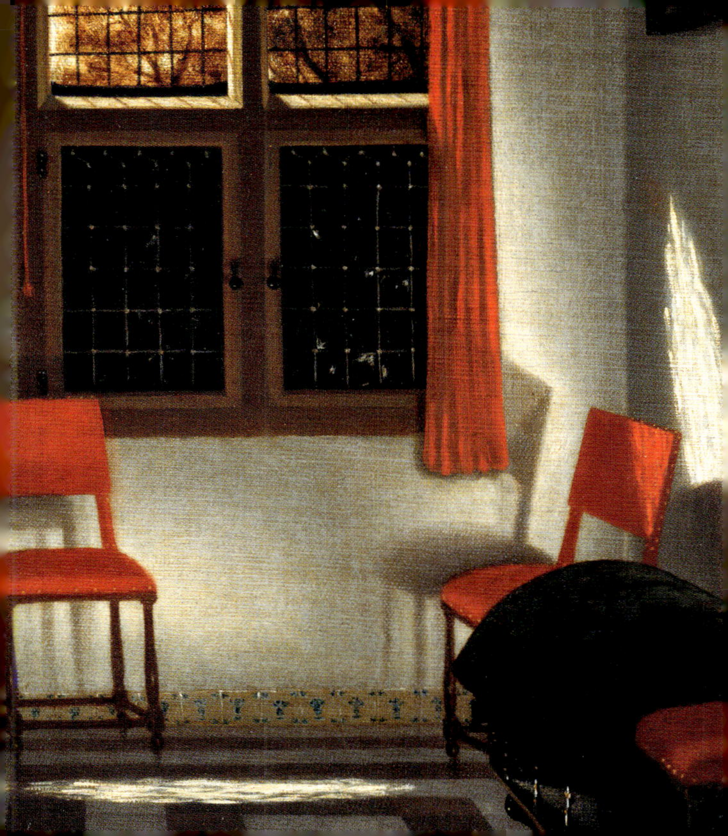

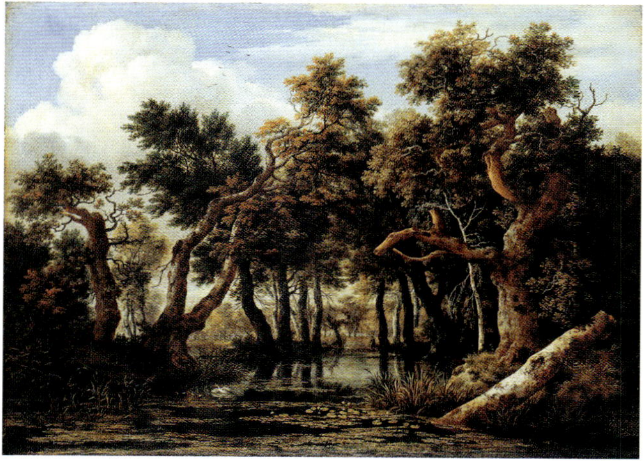

Jacob Isaaksz van Ruisdael
The Marsh
1660s. Holland

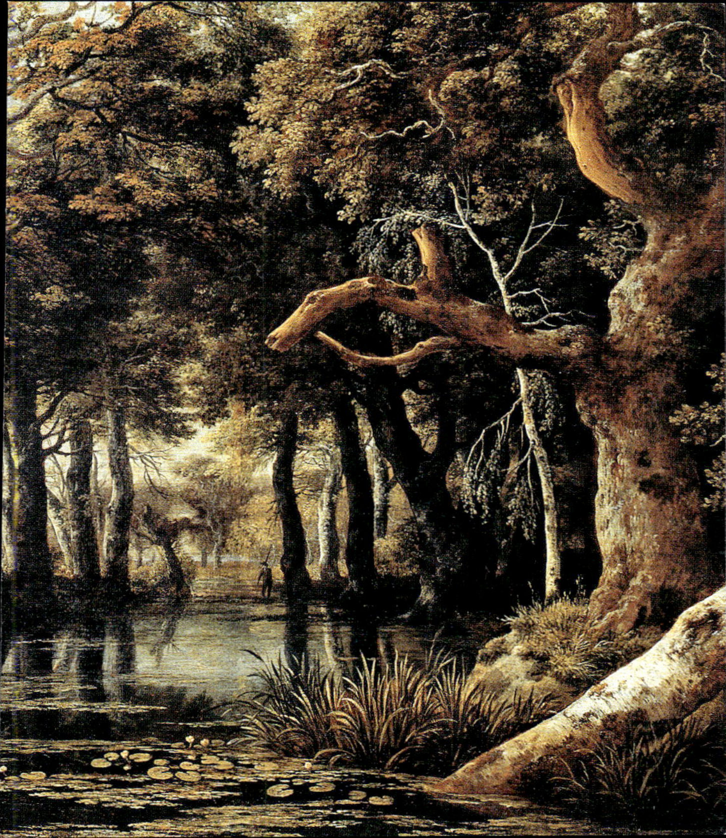

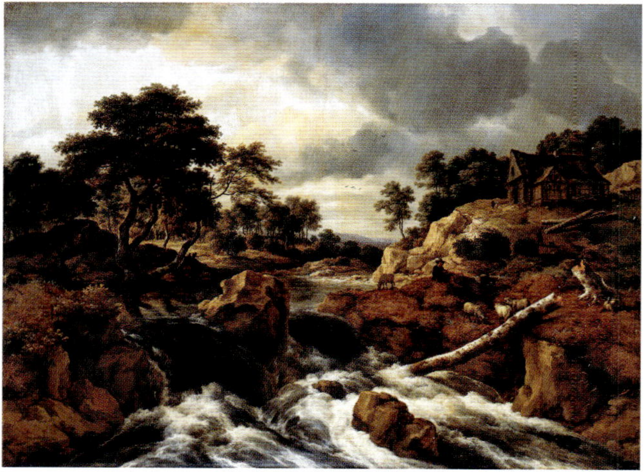

Jacob Isaaksz van Ruisdael
Waterfall in Norway
Late 1660s – early 1670s. Holland

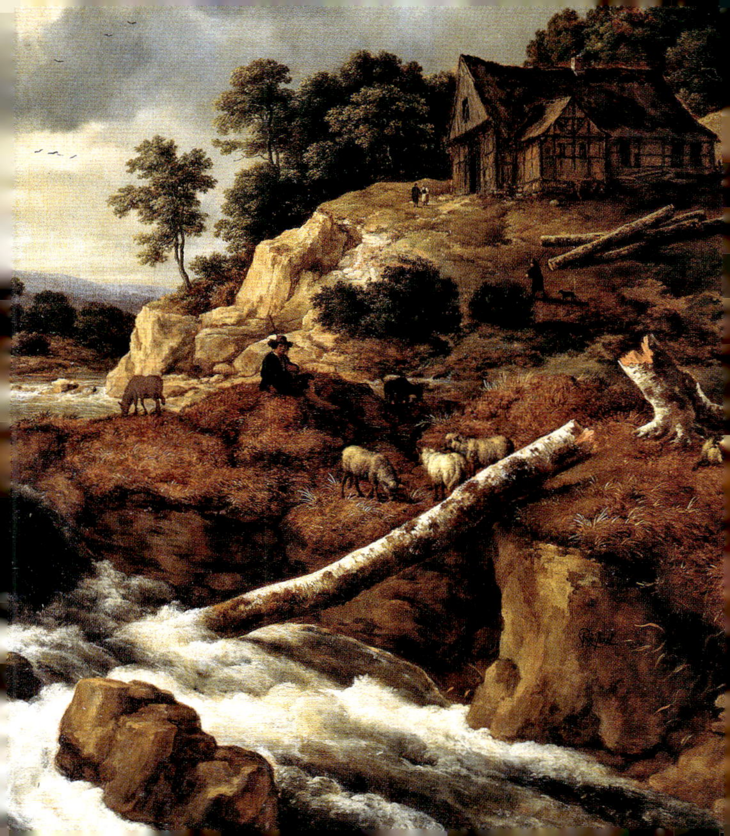

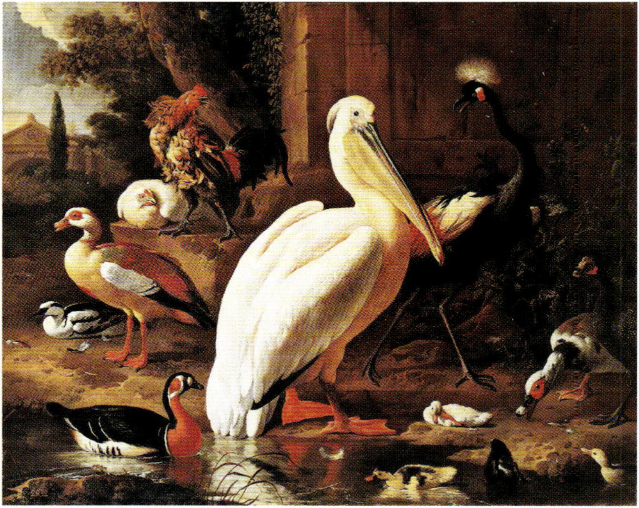

Melchior de Hondecoeter
Birds in a Park
1686. Holland

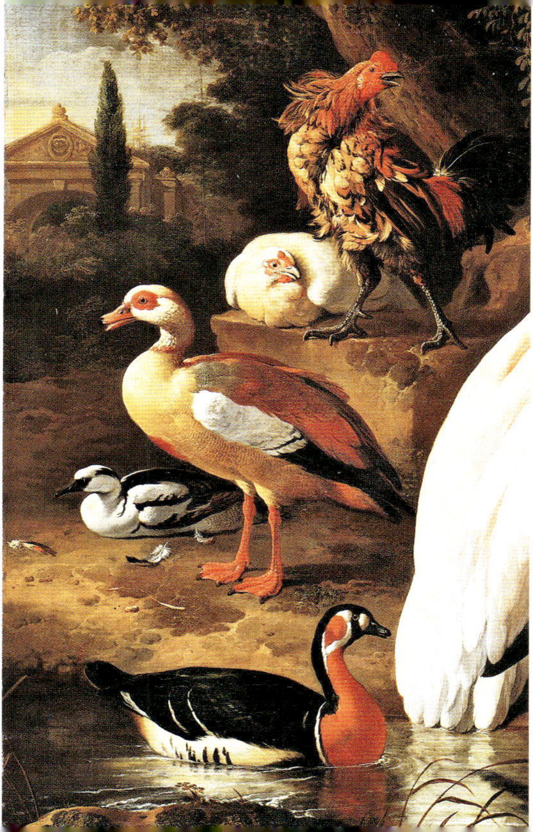

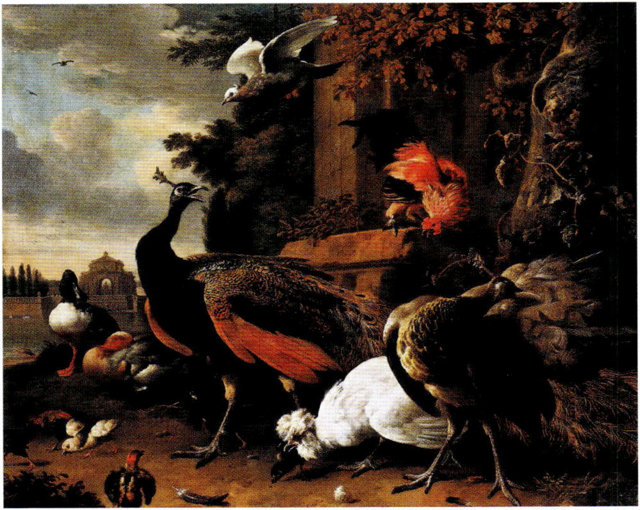

Melchior de Hondecoeter
Birds in a Park
1686. Holland

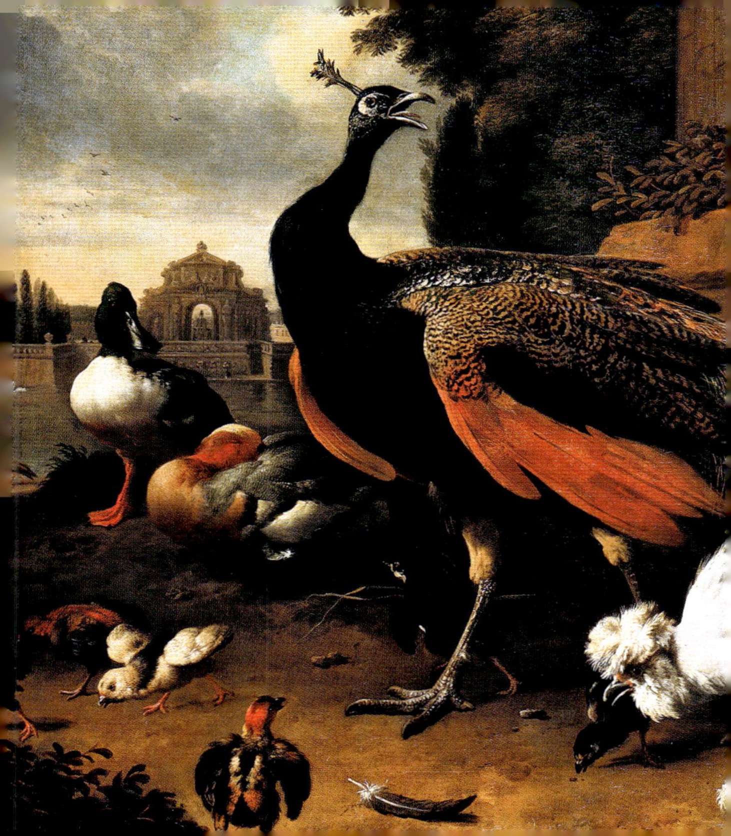

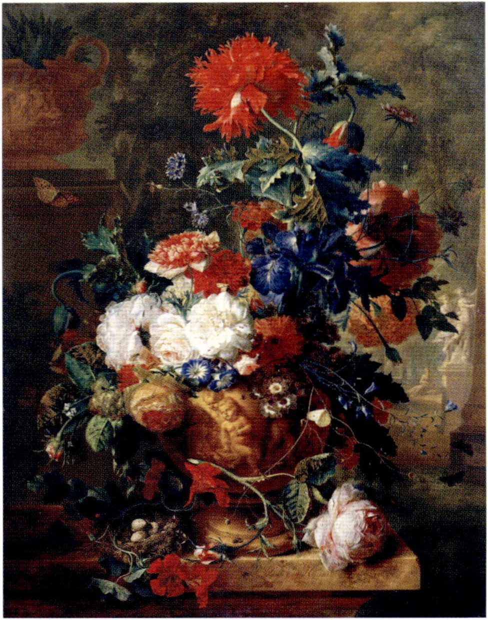

Jan van Huijsum

Flowers

1722. Holland

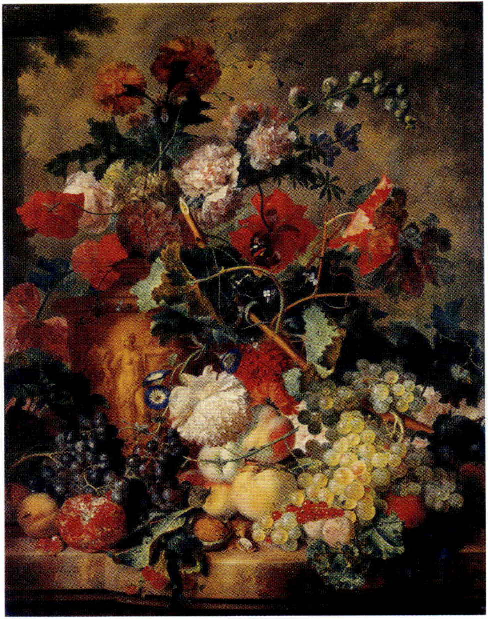

Jan van Huijsum
Flowers and Fruit
1723. Holland

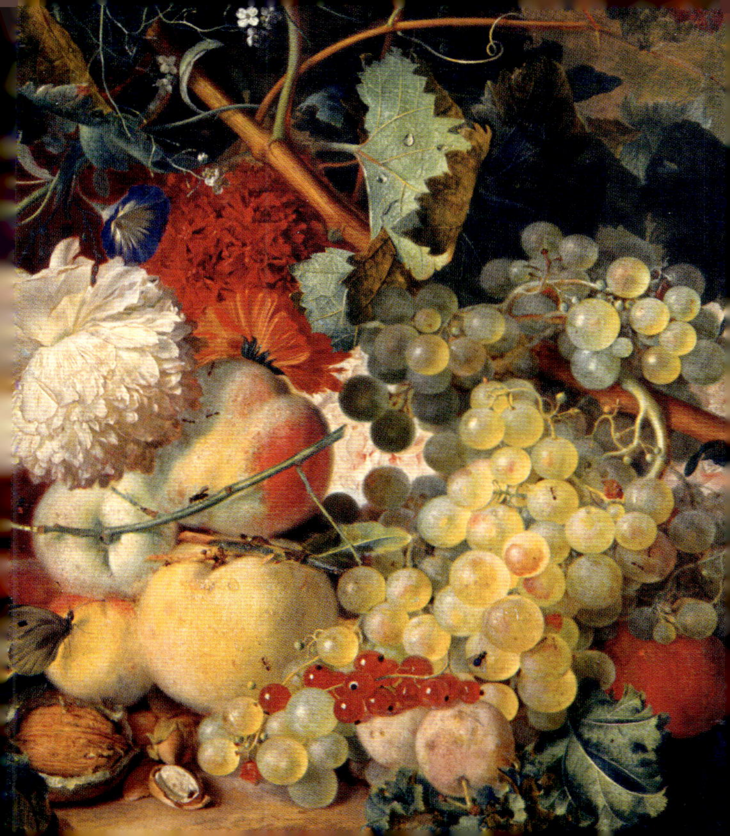

INDEX OF ARTISTS

Ast, Balthasar van der 146
Berckheyde, Gerrit Adriaensz 212
Bles, Herri Met de 56
Borch, Gerard ter 160
Brueghel, Pieter (the Younger) 80
Campin, Robert (Master of Flemalle) 6
Circle of Hieronymus Bosch 38
Claesz, Pieter 166
Cleve, Joos van 70
Coxie, Michiel van 73
Dou, Gerard 216
Droochsloot, Joost Cornelisz 206
Dyck, Anthony van 122
Geertgen Tot Sint Jans, Gerard (?) 10
Goes, Hugo van der 19
Hals, Frans 158
Heda, Willem Claesz 170
Heem, Jan Davidsz de 148
Heemskerck, Maarten van 46
Hondecoeter, Melchior de 230
Hooch, Pieter de 222
Huijsum, Jan van 234
Janssens Elinga, Pieter 224
Jordaens, Jacob 134
Kalf, Willem 172

Keyser, Thomas Hendricksz de 154
Leyden, Lucas van 60
Lijtens, Gijsbrecht (?) (Master of the Winter Landscape) 84
Mandijn, Jan 42
Master of the Female Half-Lengths 30
Master of Flemalle. See Campin, Robert
Master of the Winter Landscape. See Gijsbrecht Lijtens (?)
Neer, Aert van der 200
Ostade, Adriaen van 214
Patinir, Joachim (?) 52
Provost, Jan 24
Rembrandt Harmensz van Rijn 174
Roemerswaele, Marinus van 76
Rubens, Pieter Paul 94
Ruisdael, Jacob Isaaksz van 226
Ryckaert, David III 143
Snyders, Frans 88
Steen, Jan 218
Tempel, Abraham van den 220
Teniers, David the Younger 142
Terbrugghen, Hendrick Jansz 164
Velde, Willem van de (the Younger) 196
Vinckeboons, David 152
Weyden, Rogier van der 14
Witte, Emanuel de 156

Arca Publishers
6-8, Dvortsovaya square
St. Petersburg, 191186, Russia
Tel.: +7(812) 495-71-42
+7(812) 495-71-44
www. arcapublishers. ru

1000 copies

Printed and bound in Lithuania
Standartų Spaustuvė
39, Dariaus ir Gireno str.
Vilnius, Lithuania
www.standart.lt

EAC